HOW TO WORK WITH

LEATHER

EASY TECHNIQUES AND OVER 20 GREAT PROJECTS

KATHERINE POGSON

COLLINS & BROWN

Published in the United Kingdom in 2016 by
Collins & Brown
1 Gower Street
London
WC1E 6HD

An imprint of Pavilion Books Company Ltd

Distributed in the United States and Canada by
Sterling Publishing Co., Inc.
1166 Avenue of the Americas,
New York, NY 10036

ISBN 978-1-91116-326-8

A CIP catalogue for this book is available from the
British Library.

10 9 8 7 6 5 4 3 2 1

Reproduction by Rival Colour Ltd, UK
Printed and bound by Toppan Leefung, China

This book can be ordered direct from the publisher
at www.pavilionbooks.com

contents

introduction

I first became interested in leather when working as a theatre designer. A project I was involved in required the production of leather masks, and as I researched the process of selecting a particular type of leather and stretching it over a wooden form, I became fascinated with the sculptural properties of the substance.

Fourteen years later, I am still working with this surprising material, and enjoying teaching others some of the techniques I have explored along the way.

The most important part of any craft is good design: allowing the chosen material to speak, and working with it to produce something fresh. With leather, this often means simplicity. It is a cliché to say that every piece is unique, yet a well-designed leather product will somehow make the inherent strength, grain and beauty of its raw material seem more apparent, more real.

One of the pleasures of working with leather is that it is also incredibly long lasting. When I first began to be interested in leather design, I was very much helped and encouraged by Valerie Michael and Neil MacGregor, the leading leather crafts people in the UK. I was visiting their studio in Gloucestershire when somebody called in with a bag to be repaired. It was put on the table, gently examined and almost remembered as an old friend. The linen thread of the hand-stitched handle was just beginning to go. The bag was over twenty years old. This impressed me and has stayed with me as a standard to aspire to.

An organic material, like wood, leather continues to move and change with use, exposure to the elements and age. One of its lovely properties is that this tends to enhance it – all it needs is to be kept clean and occasionally waxed to retain its suppleness. I hope you will find as much satisfaction as I have in exploring the techniques for constructing, forming and decorating leather laid out in this book. Choose the best materials, work them lovingly and treat them well, for they may last a very long time.

leather

Many people are attracted to working with leather because of its unique quality and tactile nature. There are two ways in which leather is preserved, or tanned, to create a stable, hard-wearing substance. Each method imparts different properties to the finished product, requiring separate methods of working.

Vegetable-tanning

The traditional method of preserving leather uses tree bark, leaves and twigs. Hides are soaked in vats of tannin-rich liquid, producing strong, firm leathers such as those used for saddles, shoe soles and belts.

Classic saddle leather (undyed cow hide, also known as russet) is ideal for moulding, stamping and embossing – it can be manipulated when wet, and retains the shape once dry. It has a lovely woody smell, and a natural surface quality.

My other favourite is the gorgeous jewel-coloured goatskin produced by Harmatan and Oakridge (see page 156). A top-quality bookbinding leather with an amazing texture and grain, it is also very malleable and perfect for making brooches and three-dimensional forms.

Chrome-tanning

This method of preservation employs chrome salts and chemicals to create soft, elastic leathers that are designed to resist moisture and stretch.

Lamb nappa is a soft, springy lightweight leather mainly used for garments and light leather goods. It is available in an array of colours and finishes, foiled, printed and embossed. Soft sheep suede is good for linings and clothing, and calf or pig suede for projects requiring more strength. Chrome-tanned leathers are not suited to some of the hand decoration techniques described in this book, and can be treated much more like fabric – ideal for draping and machine stitching.

Buying leather

Purchase leather in person whenever possible, so that you can select the skins yourself (see below for sizes). Most leather will have some areas of imperfection – small holes, scratches or overstretched parts – and you may be able to work round some of these, but a poor skin will have large areas that cannot be used. Take your pattern pieces with you to check that they fit the skin. Large pattern pieces create more wastage than small ones, so it is more economical to have smaller pattern pieces joined together in panels.

Average leather sizes

Leather is sold by the complete skin or hide, or in sections of larger hides, and is graded by thickness or weight. Fashion leathers are not graded in thicknesses as hides are, but the smaller the skin the thinner the leather tends to be. The size given is for the complete surface area, and as this is not a regular shape and there may be imperfections to avoid, there is inevitably an amount of wastage. Add 20 per cent or more for wastage.

Skin: Whole skin of a small animal (sheep, pig or goat). **0.5–0.65m sq (5–7ft sq)**

Shoulder: Top section of a hide, usually cow. **0.65–1m sq (7–10ft sq)**

Side: Half a hide, usually cow or horse. **1.5–2.5m sq (15–25ft sq)**

Hide: Whole skin of a large animal (cow or ox). **2.5–5m sq (25–50ft sq)**

tools and equipment

The list of tools and equipment required for leatherworking can seem daunting. However, a small range of hand tools can be sufficient to begin with (see below) and these are relatively inexpensive. Some tools, such as solid metal punches and irons, can be fairly pricey but luckily there are ways to replicate most of their functions when you are making individual items, so that you can slowly build up your collection.

The basic requirements for leatherworking are a firm surface for cutting on, such as a solid table, a large cutting mat, a sharp knife and a couple of metal rulers with a thick edge (1 x 30cm/12in and 1 x 1m/1yd) to make cutting easier. To get started you will need specialist leatherworking tools for marking, cutting, stitching and finishing. See Resources, page 156, for a list of suppliers for tools and leather.

Essential leatherworking tools
Scribe or round (scratch) awl with long point
Rotary hole punch
Bone folder
Stitching awl with diamond-shaped blade
Single round punch
Rubber mallet and heavy metal mallet
Rivet setter (hand-held or bench-mounted)

Useful additions
Magic pen
Large round punch set
Edge-creaser or screw-creaser
Slot punch
Selection of stamping tools
Single race, groover or gouge
Safety beveller
Strap cutter
Eyelet tool
Gothic punch
Spoon and ball modelling tools
Rivet setter (bench-mounted)
Machine skiver

Essential stitching and lacing tools
Stitching awl and cork block
Pricking iron or stitching fork
Pricking wheel
Harness needles for saddle stitching
Beeswax and linen thread
Domestic sewing machine with walking foot
    and leather needle
Glover's or leather needle for hand sewing
Thonging chisel or lacing fork
Lacing needle (two-prong needle)
Lacing nippers
Single lacing chisel
Flat thonging lace or round leather lace

Waxes, dyes, glues and finishes
Carnauba cream wax
Acrylic leather paint
Saddle soap
Leather dye
Leather varnish (Tan Kote)
Antique wax (or shoe polish)
Leather glue: Impact adhesive, latex glue, paper glue,
    neoprene, rubber cement, superglue, PVA

General tools

In addition to the specialist leather tools, you will also need some general craft and hardware tools and equipment to hand in your workshop (see below). Additional equipment for each project is listed in the materials lists and you will soon begin to build a good resource.

- Scissors
- Tape measure
- Set of French curves or curved ruler
- Ordinary hand sewing needle
- Pliers
- Screwdriver
- Paintbrush, ideally a 1.5cm (½in) flat paintbrush for edge painting
- Bulldog clips (cover the grips with soft leather to protect the work)
- Staple gun and staples for moulding projects
- Bench vice and G clamps for frame setting (pad the jaws with a towel)
- Sand paper
- Masking tape
- Double-sided tape, approx 1–1.5cm (⅜–½in) wide
- Cotton cloths and sponges

Metal fittings

Metal fittings, such as Sam Brown studs, rivet studs, buckles, D-rings, key rings, bag frames and chains, eyelets and zips, can be sourced in a variety of finishes, the most common being solid brass, nickel plated and antiqued (darkened).

Vice Advice

A bench vice can also be used for setting awl blades into handles: clamp the blade sharp side down in the vice, and hammer the handle onto the end.

basic techniques

Master the key elements of cutting, gluing, edge-finishing and hole-punching and you will find you will use them in almost anything you make. Cutting a clean line is essential for good looking results. It takes practice and nerve to keep the knife upright and the pressure constant, especially on thick hides, but it is worth it! Because leather does not fray, glue is useful for constructing articles and fixing edges that will not bear too much weight. The projects in this chapter concentrate on straight lines, simple forms and finished edges, and are designed to introduce some key techniques that produce results quickly. A good example of this is scoring and folding – 'origami' style construction is still one of my favourite techniques, and a great way of creating volume quickly.

Cutting leather

1 Marking up

Leather is marked up and cut on the surface side. Avoid any scratched or marked areas and place your pattern piece onto the leather, using masking tape or weights to secure it. Draw round the shape onto the surface of the leather, or mark off measurements against a metal rule, with a scribe tool, round or scratch awl or magic pen. This is a pen that can be rubbed off after the shape is cut. Place the key pattern pieces down the centre of the leather if possible. If the chosen leather has an obvious texture or grain, work with it, keeping the grain direction consistent, and avoid any obvious diagonals.

2 Cutting out

Traditionally, leather is cut with a semicircular knife. Mastering the use of this is an art in itself. You can buy a leather or 'clicking' knife which will need regular sharpening, or use a scalpel or craft knife. A thick-sided metal ruler is required for cutting straight lines. Lay the leather out on a cutting mat on a firm surface and put your full weight onto the ruler (it may help to cut standing up). Press the knife into the cutting mat, and drag the knife towards you in one long movement. Try not to lift the knife out of the leather until the end. If you have not fully cut through, repeat the stroke from the top. It is important to keep the knife upright, especially when cutting curves. Change the scalpel blade regularly.

3 Punching holes

A rotary hole punch is a vital tool, and can be kept sharp by placing a second piece of thick leather underneath the piece you are punching. Rotate the head clockwise to change the size of the hole and hold the handle at the end for maximum leverage. Single round punches can also be bought, and are useful for making holes in areas that you cannot reach with the rotary punch. Hammer in to the leather as described in Step 5.

4 Grooving

There are many different names used to describe the grooving tool and its function, including channelling, gouging and racing. The rounded end of the groove or gouge is pressed into the leather and dragged along, to create a channel. Traditionally, saddlers set their stitches into a channel, so that they do not wear down with use. In this book, channelling or grooving is usually done on the underside of the leather, to make it fold cleanly.

5 Using a slot punch

Slot punches are most often used to create an opening to hold the prong of a buckle, allowing it to rotate (see Record Bag, page 116). Hammer the punch into the leather to create a slot. If the slot needs to be longer, move the punch up and down accordingly. If you do not have a slot punch, make a hole with a rotary or single punch at each end of the desired slot, and join the edges with a scalpel cut instead.

6 Piercing awl

Two types of awl are used in leatherwork, round awls and stitching awls. Stitching awls have a diamond-shaped blade, for opening holes when hand stitching. Place a cork block behind the work, and stab the awl through the leather. A round awl can be used instead of a scribe tool to mark the leather surface.

Side Guide

Leather has two sides: the surface (top side) is known as the 'grain side', and the rough underside is called the 'flesh side'. Leather is firmer in the centre of the hide and looser towards the edges, so choose the most appropriate area before you cut your design.

Useful tools and techniques

1 Edge-creasing

Marking a line or 'crease' around the edges of a piece of leather serves to define a shape, and is often used on straps and belts, and to create a guide for stitching or lacing holes. An edge-creaser tool works best on vegetable-tanned hides and firm leathers, and is not suitable for fine nappa or suede. Traditionally, it is heated before use, but if that is not practical, friction will help to deepen and darken the line on lightly dampened leathers. The tool shown here is an adjustable or screw-creaser. Adjust the creaser to the width you require, place one edge against the leather edge and press firmly. Single creasers are also available – mark the line first with a pair of dividers, or ruler and scribe.

2 Paring (skiving)

Many leather projects require the thickness of the leather to be pared away, especially when joining seams and turning edges. Bulk is removed by paring or shaving, to create a sloping edge. If you are producing many items, it may be worth investing in a machine or a bench-mounted edge skiver. The traditional leatherworker uses a flat angled knife, but a hand-held safety beveller will do just as well on small items. Push the safety beveller away from you – it works like peeling a potato!

3 Turning edges

Where a raw edge is not suitable, a pared or skived edge can be glued over to create a neat finish. This type of edge does not need to be top stitched, unless it will be subject to lots of wear. A turned edge is often used to hold a backing in place, as in traditional bookbinding. Prepare both surfaces with glue, and press the skived edge smoothly into place with a bone folder.

4 Smoothing edges

A bone folder is an essential tool, much used by bookbinders, that enables you to polish cut edges, burnish surfaces, smooth turned edges and press folds. Rub the dampened edge of russet leather to create friction and remove ragged fibres. Adding a watered down solution of paper glue or PVA will make the edge very shiny when burnished.

5 Burnishing

This technique is suitable for vegetable-tanned leathers only. When the dampened piece of russet is almost dry, rub the surface with a dry, clean cotton cloth in a circular motion, and it will become smooth and darken. Wax can be applied afterwards. This action seals the surface, protecting it from scratches and marks. If the leather is to be dyed (see page 99), do this when it is dry, before burnishing.

6 Waxing

Most chrome leathers will not need to be waxed as they are treated at the tannery. Vegetable-tanned and hand-dyed leathers should be waxed and sealed, especially if they will be exposed to the elements. A great many wax products exist: carnauba cream is the lightest and has a clean smell. Saddle soap has a bit more oil, and can be used with a damp cloth to clean and rehydrate old leather goods. Rub the wax evenly over the leather, let it sink in for a few minutes and then buff to a shine. Leather will lose its suppleness and become brittle with age if it is not regularly 'fed' or waxed.

Gluing

1 Surface preparation

Smooth surfaces to be joined should be scratched or sanded if necessary to create a slight roughness and to remove any varnish, wax or coating. Make some spatulas from offcuts of card. Spread a thin layer of glue on each surface, keep the coating thin and avoid the build up of lumps of glue. Go right up to the edges.

2 Applying leather

Once the glue has become touch dry, apply the leather to the surface and press together firmly. Excess glue can be rubbed off when dry. Use a bone folder to smooth the leather and eradicate any creases or bumps beneath the surface.

3 Laminating

There is a great deal of gluing involved in leatherwork! Laminating describes how two flat areas or pieces of soft leather can be joined together, as when adding a leather lining or backing. To avoid stretching and distorting the shape, glue the leathers together first with a contact adhesive spread thinly on both sides with a cardboard spreader. Press the two pieces firmly together when dry to the touch. Trim after gluing, for a more accurate shape.

Edge painting

Paint Effects

Acrylic leather dye is actually a plastic paint which sits on the surface, and is flexible enough to move with the leather. It can be effective to paint the raw flat edge of a thick hide in a contrasting colour (see Butterfly Desk Set, page 28). If you can't find the right shade of leather paint, use a standard acylic paint instead.

4 **Folding**
A bone folder has many uses. It can be used to press folds and creases in a single or double, glued piece of leather. Use a rubbing motion, to remove bulk, lumps and unevenness.

In some leathers, especially chrome-tanned fashion leathers, the dye colour does not penetrate throughout the whole skin and the cut edge appears grey. Acrylic-based paints can be used to disguise this, and to seal areas where several layers are glued together. Use a flat brush to apply the paint.

easy

★

polka frame

With simple cutting, gluing and punching, this is the perfect first project to get to grips with basic techniques. Choose two contrasting colours – a bold main colour, such as this red, will work well with both colour and black-and-white photographs. When choosing the base frame, ensure that the front has wide edges to show off the leather and give room for the polka dot pattern.

Materials

Leather: Offcuts of firm
leather in main colour,
approx. 1.6–2mm thick
(4–5oz); smaller pieces
in a contrasting colour
and same thickness.
Soft, stretchy leather is
not suitable for this
project
Wooden photo frame

Tools and equipment:
Paper or card, pencil and
ruler
Scalpel or craft knife
Cutting mat
Metal ruler
Sand paper
Acrylic leather paint
Paintbrush
Leather glue: Impact
adhesive
Bone folder
Magic pen
Scribe
Rotary hole punch
Carnauba cream wax
Cotton cloth

1 Place the frame on a piece of paper or card and draw round it. Draw in the window, to create a paper template of the frame. Design a pattern of polka dots, and draw this onto the paper on the side edges. Draw in the angles at each corner. Cut out the two side frame pieces as a template for the polka dot pattern.

2 Rub down the frame with sand paper to create a rough surface. Paint the inside rim of the frame with acrylic paint to match the main colour, if required.

3 Mark up and cut out four straight strips from the contrasting leather to match the length of each outside edge of the frame (see page 14), adding 1cm (⅜in) to each length but ensuring the width of the strip matches the exact depth of the frame.

4 Glue the top and bottom strips to the frame first, using an impact adhesive applied to both surfaces (see page 18). Trim the ends flush with the frame. Glue the side strips, so that they cover the raw edge of the leather as well as the wood. Trim the ends.

5 Measure the new height and width of the frame, with the leather attached. Cut four strips from the main colour, to match the width of the front of the frame, adding 1cm (⅜in) to each length.

6 Cut the end of the first strip at an angle to match the mitred corner of the frame. Lay the strip on the frame, measure and mark the next mitred corner and cut the strip to size. Work round the frame, matching angles and cutting each side in turn.

7 Transfer the dot design to the side strips. Lay the paper pattern piece from Step 1 on the surface of the leather, centre it, and press through the paper with a scribe to mark the position of the dots.

8 Punch out the dot design with a rotary hole punch (see page 14), remembering to use a second piece of leather behind to keep the tool sharp. Punch out some dots from the contrasting leather. You may have to punch a few before they begin to fall out of the rotary punch.

9 Glue the strips in place, and then glue the contrasting leather dots in the holes. Touch in any raw edges of leather with the acrylic paint, if required. When dry, polish lightly with carnauba cream wax (see page 17).

polka frame   23

easy
★

plaited cuff

A cuff with a twist – literally! This project looks dramatic, but is very easy to do. The thick, vegetable-tanned hide is the perfect base for practising straightforward scribing and edge-creasing, and its beautiful, warm colour is given centre stage with a little light burnishing to bring out its natural sheen. The pattern can easily be extended to make a fabulous matching belt.

Materials

Leather: Piece of vegetable-
tanned hide (russet),
0.1m sq (1ft sq),
2.5–3mm thick (6–8oz)

Tools and equipment:
Scribe or magic pen
Scalpel or craft knife
Cutting mat
Metal ruler
Edge-creaser
Bone folder
Cotton cloth
Rotary hole punch
Stamping tools and rubber
    mallet (optional)
Sam Brown stud

Template: page 146

1 Draw a rectangle 22 x 6cm (8½ x 2⅜in) on the leather with a scribe. Referring to the template on page 146, score two 16cm (6¼in) lines dividing the cuff into three equal parts in the centre, keeping edges intact. Cut out the cuff and cut the two long slits into the leather.

2 Dampen the leather slightly with cold water, then lay it on the cutting mat to absorb the water.

3 Crease a continuous line approx. 5mm (¼in) in from the edge of the leather using the edge-creaser or scribe (see page 17). Crease a line around each slit.

4 When the cuff is almost dry, burnish the edges using a bone folder and soft cotton cloth until they darken and become shiny (see page 16). Burnish the surface of the leather with an undyed cotton cloth, such as calico.

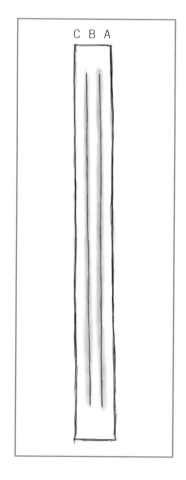

5 Label the three parts to be braided A, B and C as in the diagram.

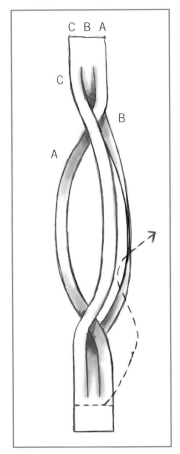

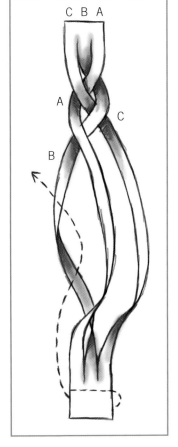

Stamp Out

If you want to decorate your cuff with a stamped design (see Cherry Compact, page 106), do this while the leather is still damp.

6 Pull strap A over strap B, under strap C and over to the left. Bring the lower end of the work through the gap between B and C.

7 The work should now look twisted as in the diagram above. Fear not!

8 Pull strap B under strap A and over to the left. Bring the lower end of the work through the gap between A and B. The cuff is magically plaited.

9 To complete the cuff fastening, insert a Sam Brown stud as described on page 75. The ends of the cuff should overlap by 3cm (1¼in), with the stud in the centre.

easy

★

butterfly desk set

In rich saddle hide, this book cover and box would look stunning adorning any desk. This project introduces neat folding techniques, and a tiny amount of hand stitching, for elegant results. The cover will fit any standard small-sized (A5) book – diary, address book or sketch pad – and the butterfly detail acts as a charming 'button' closure.

Materials

Leather: Saddle hide,
    60cm sq (2ft sq),
    2.5–3mm thick (7–8oz)

Tools and equipment:
Cutting mat
Metal ruler
Scalpel or craft knife
Scribe or magic pen
Strap cutter (optional)
Single race or grooving tool
Rotary hole punch or oval
    slot punch (optional)
Rubber mallet
Carnauba cream wax
Cotton cloth
Acrylic leather paint
Paintbrush
Stitching fork (pricking iron)
Stitching awl
Cork block
Harness needle, size 4
Waxed linen thread
Leather glue: Impact
    adhesive
3 x screw studs
Sand paper
Sam Brown stud

Template: page 146

1 Following the templates on page 146, cut out the pattern pieces for both items. Cut 2 x 11.5cm (4½in) square base pieces for the box. Mark the position of the butterfly and slot on the surface of the book and the fold lines on the inside (flesh side) of the book and box pieces with a scribe. Cut the small strap by hand, or use a strap cutter.

2 Groove or gouge a straight channel with the race tool on the inside of the leather where each fold is marked (see page 15). Make each channel no deeper than half the thickness of the leather. Test to see if the leather folds easily. Gouge the underside of the butterfly too, so it folds in half.

3 Punch the 'buttonhole' slot onto the surface of the book leather, using a slot punch and rubber mallet (see page 15). The butterfly must be able to fit easily through this when folded. If you do not have an oval punch, use a rotary punch as indicated.

4 Trim the ends of all the channels with a scalpel. Burnish the channels and all the edges including the buttonhole, to remove any roughness (see page 17) and polish the leather surface with carnauba cream and a soft cloth. Paint all the edges, using a flat brush and contrasting edge-paint (see page 19).

5 Mark stitch holes 3–5mm (⅛–¼in) in from either end of the book strip with a stitching fork and hammer. To ensure the holes are fully open, pierce through each one with the awl into the cork block, keeping the angle of the holes as marked. Place the strip in position inside the cover, transfer the markings, and pierce holes in the cover.

6 Stitch the strip in place with linen thread or strong button thread (see page 45). Pierce holes in the butterfly and book cover (see Step 5), and stitch the butterfly in position. Bring the wings together and push them through the slit to close the cover.

7 To assemble the box, punch holes where indicated on the pattern to join the sides. Glue the inner flap in place, keeping the holes aligned, and insert the screw studs (see page 32).

8 Glue the two squares wrong sides together, aligning the edges carefully. Glue this piece into the bottom of the box. Scratch the surfaces to be glued first, to make them stick better. Insert a Sam Brown stud to close the top of the box (see page 75).

Top Score

It is important to choose a firm leather for this project, and one that is thick enough to score. Place a piece of cardboard beneath the work when grooving or scoring, to protect the cutting mat, otherwise you will make gouge marks in it which make it difficult to cut on later.

easy

★

coin concertina

This cute, folded coin wallet looks fabulously chic in contrasting shades and would make a great gift for the girl about town. It is simple to create and the folding technique means there is very little construction involved. The two tiny seams at the sides can be joined either with rivets or lacing.

Materials

Leather: Soft leather (lamb nappa) for main purse, approx. 30cm sq (1ft sq), and soft leather or suede in contrasting colour for lining approx. 30cm sq (1ft sq)

Tools and equipment:
Cutting mat
Metal ruler
Scalpel or craft knife
Magic pen or scribe
Narrow single race or gouge tool
Bone folder
Leather glue: Impact adhesive
Acrylic leather paint
Paintbrush
Rubber mallet
Rotary hole punch
Hand-held rivet setter (optional)
8 x small rivet studs (optional)
Glover's or leather needle for hand sewing
Polyester thread
Button
Small length of elastic cord

Template: page 147

1 Cut out the body piece and inner pocket from the main shade, using the templates on page 147. Cut the lining piece from a contrasting colour. Mark the position of the holes, button and elastic with a magic pen or the point of a scribe. Decide whether to use rivets or thonging at the sides.

2 Groove the fold lines marked on the pattern very gently on the inside (flesh side) of the leather, using a narrow gouge or race tool. Fold the purse into the finished shape along the grooves and press firmly with a bone folder.

3 Glue the lining piece to the centre of the purse body wrong sides together (see page 18). Align the straight edges. Turn the pieces over so that the outer leather is face down, and trim the corners of the lining to match the curve of the main body. Press the folds again.

4 Paint the edges, using a flat brush and acrylic leather paint (see page 19). Mix a paint to tone with either of the leathers used.

5 Attach the sides of the inner pocket to the main body of the purse. If you are using studs, follow the steps on page 72. The studs must go through four layers of leather: the two sides of the purse and the double inner flap piece.

6 You may decide to lace the pocket in place, instead of using rivets. Punch holes as for the rivets, but cut a thin length of leather, approx. 3–4mm (⅛in) wide and use a simple whipstitch or oversewing motion to hold the edges together. Glue the ends of the lace inside the seam.

7 Add a button at point A, and a small loop of elastic to the underside of the flap at point B, to create the fastening. Use ordinary polyester thread and a Glover's needle to stitch these to the leather.

Edge Trimmer
When gluing soft leathers together, trim them to size after they have been glued, in order to get a neat edge.

coin concertina   35

intermediate
★★

origami box

This pretty jewellery box lined with Japanese origami paper introduces a new kind of leather – bookbinding goatskin – and shows how to pare and fold edges for neat results. There are many types of origami paper available, but Chiyogami paper is thicker and comes in countless beautiful designs, many with metallic embellishments and cherry blossom motifs or geometric patterns.

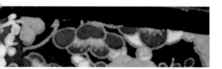

Materials

Leather: Bookbinding
  goatskin, approx.
  60cm sq (2ft sq)
Large sheet grey card,
  2mm (¹⁄₁₆in) thick
Japanese origami or
  Chiyogami paper

Tools and equipment:
Cutting mat
Metal ruler
Scalpel or craft knife
Paper glue
Superglue
Masking tape
Paintbrush
Safety beveller (optional)
Scribe or magic pen
Bone folder
Leather glue: Impact
  adhesive
Carnauba cream wax
Cotton cloth

Template: page 147

1 Cut out the five hexagons
   from the grey card,
following the template on page
147: 1 x 7cm (2¾in) radius;
2 x 6cm (2⅜in) radius;
1 x 5.5cm (2⅛in) radius;
1 x 5cm (2in) radius.

2 Cut a strip of grey card
   36.6 x 6cm (14⅜ x 2⅜in)
for the sides of the box. Score
the card into six equal sections
with the tip of the scalpel. Turn
the strip over and bend the
card either side of each score
forward, to create the wall of
the box.

3 Glue 1 x 7cm (2¾in),
   1 x 6cm (2⅜in) and
1 x 5cm (2in) cardboard
hexagons together for the lid.
The remaining 6cm (2⅜in)
hexagon will form the base of
the box. Superglue the box wall
to the base so that the hexagon
sits just inside and the score
lines on the strip face outward.
Tape all joins on both sides
firmly with masking tape.

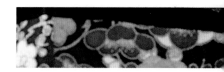

4 Cut the lining from Japanese paper, following the template on page 147. Cut a 6.5cm (2½in) radius paper hexagon to line the box lid. Cut a 9cm (3½in) radius hexagon of leather for the lid, and a 7cm (2¾in) radius leather hexagon for the base. Cut a strip of leather 38.5 x 7cm (15¼ x 2¾in), for the side.

5 Glue the paper lining for the box lid to the remaining card hexagon with paper glue, folding the paper over the edges of the card. Crease the paper box lining where indicated. Glue the base in first, using a paintbrush to spread the glue lightly over the paper. To attach the sides, begin by gluing the overlap section of one wall in place on a card fold, pulling the top edge neatly over the top of the box. Glue the next lining piece over it, and work round the box, tucking the last overlap piece behind the first piece of paper.

6 Wrap the side leather round the box – there should be an overlap of approx. 1cm (⅜in) or less. Trim any excess. Pare (skive) one edge of the leather to a depth of 1cm (⅜in) using a safety beveller or scalpel (see page 16). Pare the base leather edges to a depth of 1cm (⅜in) and the lid leather edges to a depth of 2cm (¾in). You should remove about half of the bulk of the leather.

7 Glue the base leather in place with impact adhesive. Remove a V-shaped piece of excess leather at each corner, and glue the pared (skived) leather up the wall of the box. Smooth it down with the bone folder. Glue on the leather for the box sides with impact adhesive, beginning with the pared end, positioned on one wall join. The other end should cover this neatly. Press the join with the bone folder.

8 Glue the leather to the surface of the lid with impact adhesive, and use the bone folder to define the edges of the hexagons. Remove V-shapes at the corners as before, and glue the pared area neatly over the edge of the card, using the bone folder to press and smooth. Glue the paper-lined hexagon in place on top with impact adhesive.

9 Wax the leather with carnauba cream and a cotton cloth. Cover the leather liberally with wax and let it sink in for five minutes before buffing. This will bring out the wonderful grain of the goatskin.

Hexagon by Hand

The lid of this box is decorated with a tier of three hexagons covered with leather. To make a hexagon, draw a circle and divide the circumference by the radius with a pair of compasses. Join the six points with a ruler.

stitching

Now that you have become used to handling different weights of leather, it is time to introduce stitching. This chapter will show you how to stitch both by hand and machine, and on soft and hard leathers. Begin with the ultra-simple but stylish shopper to get to grips with machine stitching, or the sandals for an introduction to the art of saddle stitching by hand. Don't be afraid of hand stitching firm leathers. It is a joy to do, very versatile, and – as the holes are made first – not hard on the hands at all!

Preparing for saddle stitching

Teething Tips

Stitching forks or pricking irons have a number of angled teeth, which allow the stitches to lie neatly. Tools with straight teeth are for lacing, not stitching, so make sure you order the correct kind. Irons come in different sizes, according to how many stitches per inch are required – 4 being the largest. Choose one with fairly wide spaced teeth to start with, or you will be stitching for a very long time!

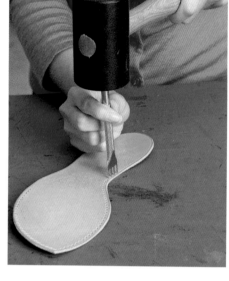

1 Creasing

Creasing is the action of impressing a line into leather. This gives you a guideline for making your stitching holes, and can be done with a pair of dividers or compasses if you do not have an adjustable creaser. Decide how far from the edge your stitches will lie, and adjust the edge-creaser tool accordingly (see page 16). Rest one side against the edge of the work and use the point to inscribe an even line on all areas to be stitched.

2 Making holes

Stitching holes are hammered into the surface of the leather with a stitching fork or pricking iron and rubber mallet. The idea is to mark the position of the holes rather than make the hole in one go, so do not try to force the tool all the way through on thick leathers. Place the first tooth in the last hole as you go along to keep the stitches even.

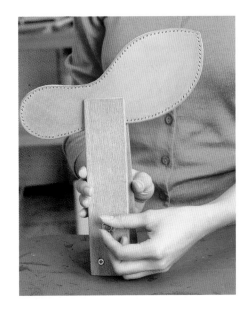

3 Working curves

To transfer stitching holes to a curved area, a pricking wheel in the same size as the iron being used is required to make sure your stitches stay the same distance apart. Place a spoke of the wheel in the last hole marked and run the wheel carefully along the line. Resume with the fork when the line is straight enough.

4 Opening the holes

A stitching awl with a diamond-shaped blade is used to open up the holes. Keep the blade upright and push it through the hole into a thick cork block, making sure you keep the angle and shape of the hole consistent. On thick leathers, check all your holes in this way, so that you do not struggle to push the needle through once you've started stitching.

5 Clamping

Saddle stitching requires both hands, so you will need a clamp to hold your work for you some of the time. The traditional saddler's 'clam' is a lovely piece of wood shaped like an enormous pair of tweezers, held between the knees. Table-mounted versions can be purchased from bookbinders, or a woodworking clamp could be adapted. If you use a metal clamp, always pad and cover the jaws with cloth or scrap leather, as iron easily stains russet leather.

 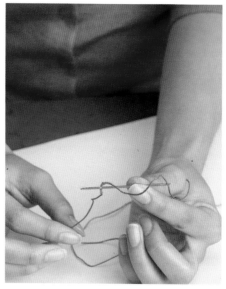 

6 Waxing thread

Linen thread is used for saddle stitching, and needs to be waxed before use, to keep it clean and make it pass more easily through the work. The thread should be four times longer than the distance to be stitched. Cut the thread and pull it through a block of beeswax several times.

7 Threading needle

Hand stitching for large projects is done with strong, blunt-pointed harness needles. Choose a needle with an adequate sized eye for the thread being used – I usually use size 4. Thread the needle, and then untwist the thread slightly below the needle. Pass the needle through the middle of the thread.

8 Securing thread

Pull on the short end of the thread, and tighten up the loop. You have now secured your needle without creating a knot. Without this trick, the pulling motion of stitching will make the needles fly off, requiring endless rethreading.

Backstitch

This is a useful stitch for decorative stitching, or projects where only one side of the work is visible. Bring the needle through the second hole from the back and into the first from the top. Bring the needle out through the third hole and back through the second. Continue in this way, and finish off by oversewing through two or three stitches on the back side when complete.

Saddle stitch

1 Starting stitching

Saddle stitching requires two harness needles at the same time, one on either end of the thread. The method shown here is a simplified version of the traditional method (where the holes are pierced with the awl as you work). If two wrong sides are being stitched together, as with the strap shown here, one set of holes must be marked on the inside (flesh side) of the leather, or they will not match up. Thread the needles, place your work in a clamp and push one needle through the first stitch hole, finding the centre of your length of thread. Push the first needle into the second hole, and pull down to the bottom of the angled hole.

2 Working two needles

Bring the second needle through from the other side above the first and pull tight with an upward motion. Then place this needle into the next hole and pull down. Repeat this process, trying to keep the rhythm and tension consistent as you stitch, so that the thread lies evenly between the angles of the holes.

Machine stitching

Fine and lightweight leathers can be sewn on an ordinary domestic sewing machine with a few simple adaptations – a leather needle and a Teflon-coated or walking foot (metal feel cause leather to stretch and create drag marks). The main point to consider in machine sewing leather is the thickness of the material, the edges often need to be pared or skived first. If you try to sew leather that is too thick, you will eventually burn out the machine motor, so if you are considering batch production, it may be worth investing in an industrial or cylinder arm leather machine. Having selected suitably thin leather, choose a longer stitch than you would normally use on fabric, adjusting the length to compensate for the thickness of the material.

3 Overlapped seam

The stitching method for an overlapped seam is the same as already described, but the holes will both be made on the grain side or surface of the leather. This kind of seam can be lightly glued together with PVA as it is difficult to clamp.

4 Finishing off

You do not need to tie a knot, because the double stitching action is incredibly strong. Simply stitch back over the last two or three stitches and cut the thread off close to the surface – it will not unravel if it has been properly stitched.

Test Runs

Do some stitch length tests on scraps first – if the stitch is still not even after playing with the stitch length, try loosening the pressure of the foot. The next step after that is to gradually loosen the tension.

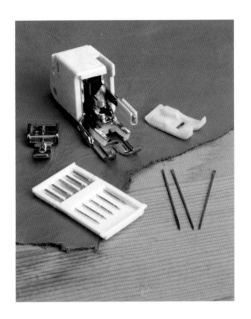  

1 Equipment

A walking foot is a very useful investment. This adaptation is attached to the post, and feeds the material evenly between the dogs under the needle. Teflon feet are cheaper and useful for top stitching, or a Teflon coating can be stuck onto the underside of existing metal feet, such as a zipper foot. You will also need leather machine needles with blade-like tips, which cut into the surface of the leather. Use ordinary polyester threads for a domestic machine, as the heavier kinds of nylon threads for leather will not suit the machine or needle. Use bulldog clips to hold the edges together, instead of pins.

2 Straight stitch seam

Stitch a straight seam exactly as you would for fabric, but remember that the needle's holes will show if you have to rip out, so draw a line to follow if necessary, and go very slowly! If you do rip out and try to re-sew a line, you may find that the leather rips along the perforation. The turnings of flat seams can be glued and gently hammered or boned in place instead of ironed, or the seam allowance can be trimmed away if necessary. Thread ends are worked in by hand as normal.

3 Overlapped seam

This seam is stronger than the straight seam, and needs a wider seam allowance of 2cm (¾in). Sew the seam as usual, and then trim one seam allowance to 1cm (⅜in). Open the seam out flat, fold both seam allowances to one side, and lightly glue the longer one over the shorter. Turn the work right side up, and topstitch 1cm (⅜in) from the fold. The fold edge can also be top stitched to give the look of a jeans seam.

Machine zigzag stitch

Roll Up, Roll Up

To create a neat edge when two pieces of leather have been sewn together on the wrong side: take the edge between the finger and thumb and roll it until the stitch line appears. Always trim the seam before turning the piece right side out, to get rid of any excess bulk.

1 Preparing strips

This is a good way to join very lightweight leathers for a decorative or patchwork effect, avoiding any bulky seams. Tape the pieces to be joined together edge to edge using masking tape. The tape will be left in place after stitching, so the work will need to be lined.

2 Joining

Make sure your walking foot is suitable for zigzag stitching – there should be a slot to allow the needle to swing from side to side. Select a wide stitch and machine down the centre join so that the zigzag is even on either side.

Making a piped seam

1 Inserting piping

A piped seam adds a professional look to many projects. As it adds more bulk to a seam, make sure your machine can handle it. Pare or skive the leather where possible, or use thinner leather for the piping. Select some cord of the desired width, measure the circumference and add 2cm (¾in). To keep bulk to a minimum, you may choose to cut the cord slightly shorter than the actual seam length required, but make the leather strip the correct length, so that the piping becomes 'empty' just before each end. Glue the strip round the cord, and press firmly with a bone folder. Using a Teflon-coated foot, sew the piping together.

2 Joining piped seams

Place the piping right sides together against one of the pieces to be joined. Tuck the piping end without cord inwards to avoid too much bulk at the edge. When sewn together the piping is 'lost' just before the seam end. Hold in place with bulldog clips and sew as before. Some curved seams may require clipping first.

3 Joining pieces

Lay the second pattern piece on top and sew the pieces together, using a Teflon-coated zipper foot to enable you to stitch as close as possible to the cord. Trim away any excess bulk from the seams.

Happy Feet

A Teflon-coated zipper foot glides over the surface of the leather, whereas metal feet will drag, stretch and scar the surface.

easy

★

stripy purse

This project is a great way to use up small scraps of soft leather left over from other projects, for pretty and economical results. The zigzag stitched seams are really straightforward on the machine and you can have lots of fun with contrast stitching to make a truly individual addition to your handbag.

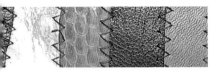

Materials

Leather: Main colour lamb nappa or suede for back and flap, 30cm sq (1ft sq), plus scraps of contrasting colours or textures of soft lamb nappa or suede, including a metallic one if possible
Lining fabric, 25cm sq (9¾in sq)

Tools and equipment:
Cutting mat
Metal ruler
Scalpel or craft knife
Masking tape
Domestic sewing machine, fitted with walking foot, leather needle
Polyester thread
Scissors
Bone folder
Leather glue: Impact adhesive
Magnetic clasp

Template: page 148

1 From the main colour, cut out a rectangle of leather for the purse body 18.5 x 22cm (7¼ x 8½in) and two strips 11 x 2.5cm (4¼ x 1in), and two strips 11 x 1.5cm (4¼ x ½in). Cut seven contrasting strips from a mixture of colours, each 11 x 1.5cm (4¼ x ½in). Cut four small 2.5cm (1in) squares from scraps – these will reinforce the magnetic clasp.

2 Place the nine 1.5cm (½in) strips in sequence, raw edges together, and carefully tape together on the back, so that the joins are flat and the masking tape does not overlap. Add the two wider strips, one either end, to make a panel measuring 18.5 x 11cm (7¼ x 4¼in). Draw a line 1cm (⅜in) in from the edge around the back, for the seam allowance.

3 Set up your sewing machine for zigzag sewing. Select an open zigzag stitch (width 3–4, length 4–5), wide enough to comfortably cover the join between strips. Do some tests to check the tension is correct, and zigzag the strips together on the right side.

4 Mark the 1cm (⅜in) seam allowance on the flesh side of the main piece. Draw a line 6.5cm (2½in) from the short edge to define where the flap will fold to become the lining.

5 Reset the machine to a slightly longer straight stitch (3–4) than you might use on fabric. Fold the flap for the back panel along the drawn line, with right sides together. Stitch straight up either side of the fold to create the lined flap. Trim the seams and corners with a sharp pair of scissors.

6 Fold over the 1cm (⅜in) seam allowance of one long edge of the stripy panel, and press flat with the bone folder. Position it directly beneath the flap on the front with right sides together. Stitch around the three edge seams, on the marked line.

7 Trim the corners, and cut all seam allowances down to 5mm (¼in). Turn the purse right side out, and roll the seams to make the edges flat. Repeat this process for the flap. You may gently press through a cotton tea towel using a moderate iron if necessary, but be careful not to shrink the leather.

8 Before inserting the magnet into the purse, reinforce the leather by gluing on the extra squares, one on the reverse of the front panel, and one on the reverse of the flap lining. Insert the two parts of the magnet (see page 77). The 'male' part goes on the flap and the 'female' on the body of the purse. Glue another square over each when fixed to protect the leather.

9 Cut out a piece of lining fabric, 18.5 x 22cm (7¼ x 8½in). Reset your machine for fabric sewing, fold in half right sides together and sew the side seams. Trim the seam, clip the corners and insert it into purse. Attach it by fitting it under the flap and front turning allowance and top stitch it in place around both the front and back.

intermediate
★★

sandal style

This is a great opportunity to make use of the kaleidoscope of colours available in soft fashion leathers for the ankle straps. You can practise your new found hand and machine stitching skills, finding your own way to adapt these stylish sandals for a truly bespoke finish.

Materials

Leather: Half a shoulder of tan belt leather or russet cowhide, 0.55m sq (6ft sq), 3–4mm thick (8–10oz)
Strips of coloured soft fashion leather, 60 x 30cm (2 x 1ft)

Tools and equipment:
Card, pencil and ruler
Scalpel or craft knife
Cutting mat
Sand paper
Leather glue: Rubber cement
Rubber mallet
Beeswax or carnauba cream
Slot punch
Scribe
Edge-creaser
Pricking iron (stitching fork)
Pricking wheel
2 x harness needles, size 4
Stitching awl
Waxed linen thread
Double-sided tape
Bone folder
Rotary hole punch
Domestic sewing machine, walking foot, leather needle
Sam Brown stud
Ordinary hand sewing needle
Paper glue

Template: page 148

1 Place your feet on a piece of card and draw round them. Simplify the shape, until you come up with a smooth outline, or adapt the template on page 148. Mark the gap between the big and second toe, and where the straps tuck under the sole as shown on the template. Cut out the shape. Add 3mm (⅛in) around the edge, and cut out a second shape. Define the heel shape, trace this onto a new piece of card and cut out. These are your three templates.

2 Mark up and cut out two of the larger soles from the main leather, then turn the template over and cut two more. Cut one of each of the smaller soles. Cut three heel shapes for each foot.

3 Scratch or sand paper the surface or grain side of two heel pieces to create a rough surface. Glue the flesh or underside of one to the scratched surface of the other. Glue the flesh side of the last, unscratched piece to the scratched surface of the second piece. Scratch the heel area only on the surface of one of the larger soles, and glue the whole heel section to this. Repeat for the other foot.

4 Hammer the glued pieces with a mallet to compress them and make sure they are firmly stuck. If you think the sandals will be subject to robust wear, you can staple through the sole into the heel with a staple gun using 6mm (¼in) staples for extra strength.

5 Burnish the edges and surfaces of the two smaller soles, and wax if desired. Use a narrow 1.5cm (½in) slot punch to make the holes where the straps will go, making sure these are more than 5mm (¼in) away from the edge, so as not to interfere with the line of the stitching.

6 Follow the steps for hand stitching on pages 42–45, beginning with creasing a line round each piece 3mm (⅛in) in from the edge. Backstitch all round each sole using a linen thread in a colour to match the straps.

7 Place the smaller sole template onto the surface of the remaining large sole and draw around it, so that you have a line 3mm (⅛in) in from the edge. Scratch or sand paper inside this line to roughen the surface.

8 Cut two strips of soft leather 18 x 3cm (7 x 1¼in) for the front straps, and two 45 x 3cm (18 x 1¼in) for the ankle straps. Draw a line down the centre of each strap on the flesh side and place a strip of double-sided tape over it. Stick the sides down to the centre line marked, and press firmly with a bone folder to make a 1.5cm (½in) wide strap. Machine stitch along each edge of the strap using a straight stitch (see page 47).

9 Tape the straps temporarily in place through the slot and under the sides of the leather, and try on the sandals, adjusting the length of the straps as necessary. Trim off any excess length, and pare away any bulk that will lie under the sole.

10 Glue the straps to the underside of the sole, and then glue the whole to the larger sole already prepared. Glue this piece to the sole and heel part, aligning the edges as carefully as possible. Wax the edges with carnauba cream and compress with the bone folder.

11 The ankle strap simply wraps round the ankle and is held in place by a tiny Sam Brown stud (see page 75). Adjust for size, and trim by cutting at an angle. Oversew the stitched edges with a hand sewing needle two or three times. If you prefer, you could add a second ankle strap on the other side of the foot and tie the straps together ribbon-fashion.

12 Rub the edges of the sandals with a mixture of paper glue and water, and burnish with a damp cloth, bone folder and a lot of elbow grease. Try to fuse the layers together as much as possible.

13 If the finished sandals are a bit uneven at the edges, and you have done all the burnishing you can, cheat by taking them to a shoe menders and asking them to machine-polish the edges for you!

Sharp Slice

As this type of leather is thick, start with a sharp blade, and try very hard to keep the knife upright in order to avoid cutting a sloping edge.

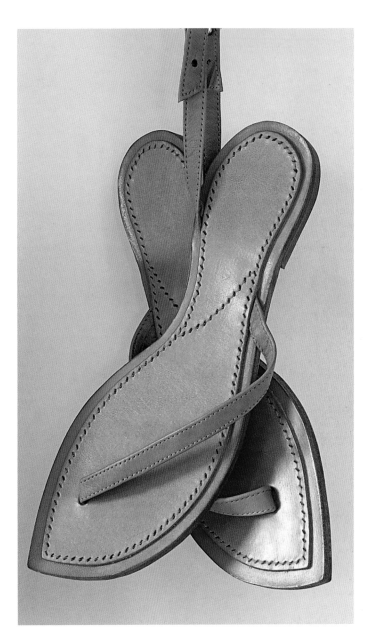

advanced

★★★

pretty in pink

I like designing three-dimensional products that are made from a single sheet of leather. This bag follows the principles of scoring and folding outlined in the Butterfly Desk Set project (see page 28), so there is only one seam. Choose a coloured linen thread to show off your prowess at hand stitching!

Materials

Leather: Coloured cow hide
  shoulder, 2–2.5mm thick
  (5–6oz)

Tools and equipment:
Card, pencil and ruler
Scalpel or craft knife
Large cutting mat
Scribe or round (scratch) awl
Rotary hole punch
French curves or curved ruler
Grooving tool (single race or
  gouge)
Bone folder
Acrylic leather paint
Paintbrush
Pricking iron
Rubber mallet
Stitching awl
Cork block
2 x harness needles, size 4
Waxed linen thread
Piping cord, 1.2m (4ft)
Leather glue: Impact adhesive
  or PVA
Bulldog clips
Sand paper
Sam Brown stud
Carnauba cream wax, cloth

Template: page 148

1 Make a card pattern using the template on page 148. Mark up and cut out the leather, including two handles and one tab piece. You may need a large cutting mat for this. Scribe the position of the tab closure, handles and stud fastening onto the surface (grain side) of the leather.

2 Score the straight fold lines on the under or flesh side of the leather with a round (scratch) awl or scribe and ruler. Mark and score the curved lines using a set of French curves (or any convenient semicircular shape you can find) to create a smooth even line.

3 Groove (gouge or channel) the score lines into the flesh side of the leather (see page 15). The grooves should go through about half the thickness of the leather. Bend the folds to check you have gone deep enough, and smooth down the outside with the bone folder. Go slowly on the curved grooves as it is easy to slip. Find something curved to lean against if possible, such as a large pan lid.

4 Trim any rough ends with a scalpel, and rub the grooves down with a damp cloth until they are smooth. Burnish all the cut edges, including the tab and straps, to remove any roughness. Paint the edges with acrylic leather paint.

5 Follow the instructions on pages 42–44 to prepare the tab to be stitched. The stitching holes should be made on the grain side of the leather. Position the tab on the bag and mark through the holes onto the bag. Press the stitching awl through the leather into a cork block placed beneath to make the holes. Stitch the tab to the bag, using backstitch.

6 Prepare the handles to be stitched, following the saddle stitch instructions on pages 45–46. Note that the stitching holes around the pointed end and along one side should be made on the surface, but along the other straight side, the stitch holes should be marked on the flesh side or underside of the leather, as shown on the template.

7 Cut two 58cm (23in) lengths of piping cord, and glue onto the underside of the handles. Hold the edges of one handle together lightly with PVA and bulldog clips, and begin saddle stitching the straight parts of the handle together. Note that the stitches stop a short way before the shaped end. Stitch the other handle.

8 To attach the handles to the bag, scratch or sand paper the triangle areas marked on the bag and lightly glue one handle end in place. Pierce through the holes already made into a cork block as before. The sides of the V will curve in as they get closer to the handle, so mark these holes accordingly on the bag. Stitch the handle to the bag with backstitch. There

may be one or two stitches just before the handle stitching, which cannot be stitched down to the bag. Backstitch through these singly to keep the look of the stitching consistent on the outside, and continue up to meet the stitching of the handle. Attach the other end and repeat for the other handle.

9 The side join of this bag uses two types of stitching in one seam: an ordinary seam and an overlapped part. Make sure you make the holes on the correct side of the leather for each (see page 46). Mark and pierce the stitching holes along the side seam, following the template on page 153. Stitch the overlapped seam up to its end, and then place both leather surfaces together and

sew the rest of the seam on the wrong side with your hands inside the bag. Repeat at the top of the other side of the bag, as shown on the template, making the tops of the bag 'gussets' fold inwards.

10 The two base pieces of the bag fold over each other and are glued together. Sand paper one of the curved surfaces, and glue it firmly to the flesh side of the other with rubber cement or a strong impact adhesive. Covering the whole surface area evenly with glue should hold the bag firmly, but you may want to add screw studs or feet for extra strength (see pages 73 and 75). If you are very dedicated you can hand stitch the base seam as well!

11 Insert the Sam Brown stud into the body of the bag (see page 75). Pull the tab closure over to the front of the bag, and mark the position of the buttonhole opening. Make the buttonhole opening in the centre, with the slit facing away from the pointed end of the tab.

12 Wax and polish the finished article with a light coat of carnauba cream.

Hidden Extras

Adding an internal zip pocket can be a handy addition to this design: make a flat pocket from soft leather, 15 x 20cm (6 x 7¾in), add a zip (see page 130), and hand stitch in place on the inside back of the bag between the points of the handles. Make the stitching holes while the project is still flat, before stitching up the side seams.

easy

★

soft shopper

This is my version of the eco-shopping bag. Shaped just like an actual plastic carrier bag, it is unlined, very simple to make and will roll up compactly to fit into a corner of your handbag. Choose a gorgeous soft lambskin or suede in a glowing colour for truly luxurious results.

Materials

Leather: Two skins of soft
   lamb nappa or suede,
   0.5–0.65m sq (5–7ft sq)
Plastic carrier bag

Tools and equipment:
Scalpel or craft knife
Card, pencil and ruler
Large cutting mat
Domestic sewing machine,
   walking foot, leather needle
Polyester thread
Glover's or leather needle for
   hand stitching
Leather glue: Impact adhesive

1 Cut the plastic bag across the handle tops, down the sides and across the base to take it apart into two equal pieces. Flatten one out on a sheet of card, and draw around the shape. Allow for any plastic cut away, and add 1cm (⅜in) seam allowance at the handles, sides and base.

2 Cut out the card pattern and lay it down the spine of the leather. Mark up and cut out one piece from each skin, keeping the grain matching.

3 Lay the two leather pieces right sides together, and sew up the side, handle and base seams with a straight stitch (see page 47). Trim the seam allowance on the side seams if desired.

4 Mark a point approx. 5cm (2in) in from each side seam at the base of the bag on the seam allowance. Fold the sides of the bag in to meet the points.

5 With a Glover's or leather needle, stitch through the seam allowance along the 5cm (2in) fold, attaching it to the base of the bag with loose oversewing stitches. This will give the bag shape and volume when full.

6 Turn the bag the right way out. Join the two sides of each handle, using an overlapped seam (see page 47), and top stitch for extra strength.

7 Roll the base seam, tuck the sides in and press flat with a moderate iron through a dry tea towel to keep the crisp plastic bag shape. Be careful when ironing leather – always try a test piece first to set the temperature, as it can shrivel very quickly with heat.

Shoulder Straps

This bag also works very well if you lengthen the handles so it can slip over the shoulder. Choose two large lambskins of similar size, lay the pattern at the bottom of the leather and cut the straps as long as you can. There will be enough leather left over to make a smaller item, such as the make-up bag on page 86.

advanced
★★★

disco diva

A piped seam adds style to any project. In this design, the curved panels at the front create the volume of the bag, and the piping emphasizes the shape even more – creating a glamorous party bag that's strong and chic enough to take to the dancefloor!

Materials

Leather: Two sides of metallic
   chrome-tanned cowhide, or
   equivalent lambskin,
   0.75–1m sq (8–10ft sq)
Iron-on interfacing, 0.5m
   (½yd)
Lining fabric, 0.5m (½yd)

Tools and equipment:
Card, pencil and ruler
Scalpel or craft knife
Cutting mat
Magic pen
Piping cord, 3m (10ft)
Leather glue: Impact adhesive
Bone folder
Bulldog clips
Magnetic clasp
Domestic sewing machine,
   Teflon-coated zipper foot,
   leather needle
Polyester thread
Ordinary hand sewing needle
Acrylic leather paint (optional)
2 x 5cm (2in) silver O-rings
12 x small rivet studs
Rotary hole punch

Template: page 149

1 Make a pattern from card
   following the template on
page 149. You should have one
pattern piece for the back of
the bag, three for the front, a
side placket, a tab closure and
a facing piece.

2 Mark up and cut out the
   leather, avoiding any
stretchy areas for the bag
pieces. Cut: 1 x main body
piece; 2 x side plackets;
2 x tab closures; 2 x facings;
2 x 24 x 3cm (9¼ x 1¼in)
strips for the seam piping;
3 x 1m x 3cm (1yd x 1¼in)
strips for the handle.

3 If you choose a lightweight
   skin, back or reinforce
all the leather pieces with
interfacing before sewing,
to strengthen them. Cut the
interfacing 1cm (⅜in) smaller
all the way round than the
leather so that it sits inside the
seam allowance. Iron it onto
the back of the leather with a
moderate heat (see page 136).

If you choose a heavier weight
cow hide, omit this step, but
pare or skive the seams to a
depth of 1cm (⅜in), especially
the facing seams, as shown on
page 16. If the cut edge of the
leather needs to be disguised,
paint the edges of the placket
and tab pieces.

4 Follow the steps on page
   49 to make up two lengths
of piping. Cut the cord approx.
2cm (¾in) shorter than the
length of the seam. Cut three
90cm (3ft) lengths of cord, and
cut three more 1m (1yd) strips
of leather for the handle. Make
up and stitch the three strips
into piping as before, leaving
about 5cm (2in) of the long
strips 'empty' of cord at either
end, so that you can join them
more easily to the rings.

5 Assemble the two piped
   seams (see page 49).
Trim the seams and ends of
the piping, and roll the seam
to define the curve.

6 Apply interfacing to both
   tab closure pieces, cutting
it slightly smaller than the tab
so it does not show at the edge.
Mark the position of the
magnetic clasp on the front of
the bag, and one of the tab
closure pieces, and insert them
as shown on page 77.

7 Place the two tab closure
   pieces wrong sides
together, and machine stitch
close to the raw edge with the
zipper foot. Paint the raw edge
if necessary. Machine stitch
the tab to the back piece of
the bag where indicated on
the template.

8 Attach the side plackets,
   which will hold the rings
for the handles in place. These
are placed on each side seam,
7cm (2¾in) below the top. Glue
the O-rings in place (see page
73). Then lightly glue the
placket to the bag and machine
stitch round the raw edge and
across the top. (You could also

add some rivet studs for extra strength, as shown on page 72.)

9 Place the back and front of the bag pieces right sides together and machine sew round the outside 1cm (⅜in) in from the edge. Clip the curves and trim the seams. Turn the bag right side out and roll the edges.

10 Cut out two pieces of lining fabric, using the back template as a pattern. Lay one piece right side up and place one leather facing piece right side up on top of it, aligning the top edges. Sew along the lower raw edge to attach it to the lining. Repeat for the other side.

11 Place the two pieces right sides together and sew the side seams as above, but leave a 12cm (4¾in) hole at the bottom of the bag for bagging out. This is the process of sewing round the top of the bag and pulling it

through the lining hole to ensure a neat top edge. The hole is hand stitched closed afterwards (see page 138).

12 Clip the curves and trim the seams of the lining up to the hole, but do not trim the leather facings, glue these seams flat open instead.

13 Place the bag inside the lining piece so that the right sides are together. Align the side seams and top with bulldog clips, and stitch all round the top, joining the two pieces. Clip and trim the seam, especially any bulk in the side seam.

14 Pull the bag through the hole in the lining, turning it right side out. Push the lining down into the bag. Roll the top, and press with the bone folder to create a neat edge. For extra definition, top stitch the edge. Sew up the hole in the lining by hand.

15 Paint the raw edges of the three handle strips if necessary. Attach three strips to one of the O-rings: bend the empty end of each piping strip round the ring in turn, glue in place with a turning of 2cm (¾in), and rivet together with

a rivet stud (see page 72). Make sure the turnings are on the inside. Plait the strips together, and attach the other ends to the opposite ring.

metal fittings

Metal fittings are both decorative and structural, and mostly simple and very quick to apply – let the fun commence! The projects in this chapter display a wide range of functions – the hardware on the patent belt looks functional but is mostly decorative. You will find other examples and applications dotted through other projects, too (see the Record Bag on page 120). The equipment required for most of these examples is inexpensive and remember it is much quicker than hand stitching, so if you are full of design ideas and short on patience, grab a hole punch and some studs and start experimenting!

Rivet studs

1 Making holes
Rivet studs are made up of two parts. The key to choosing the correct rivet is to look at the length of the shank as well as the dimensions of the head. Think about the layers of thickness the rivet will be passing through, and measure accordingly. Select a hole size that will comfortably accommodate the head of the rivet, and punch the hole with a rotary hole punch.

2 Inserting
Insert the long shank from the back of the work upwards, and click the head into place on the front side.

3 Setting
Place the joined studs into the setter or riveter, and exert firm pressure. It is worth investing in a proper bench-mounted riveter if you will be making projects regularly, as these really do fix the studs firmly in place. For lighter work, a hand-held rivet setter can be used.

D-rings

Screw studs

1 Preparing the strap

D-rings are useful for attaching handles and straps to bags, and for creating certain types of belt fastening. It may sound obvious, but it is important to measure the inner width of a D-ring before you design a project so that the strap fits! Pare the edge of the strap before attaching it to the main body of the work.

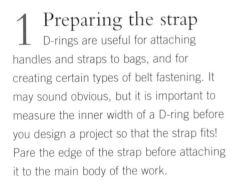

2 Securing the strap

Thread on the D-ring and scratch the area where the placket will be fixed, and glue in place. Rivet studs can be used for added strength, but it is always stronger to stitch a placket in place if it is to support a strap and the full weight of a large bag.

Another simple two-part stud, screw studs are permanently fixed in place by tightening with a screwdriver, and are especially useful when joining two thick pieces of hide.

Eyelets

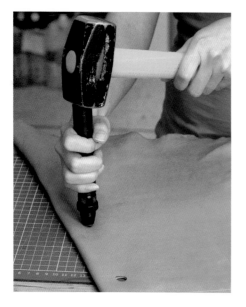

1 Punching a hole

Eyelets are fixed in a similar way to rivet studs, and also require a special tool. Measure the diameter of the eyelet and make a correspondingly sized hole with a hole punch. If your eyelets are large you may need to buy an extra large hole punch set.

2 Placing eyelets

Discard any misshapen eyelet pieces, because they can buckle and are very difficult to remove once inserted. The long eyelet piece looks best on the front of the work because it does not risk being damaged by the hammer. Place the eyelet in the holder, and the shank through the hole from the surface side to the back. Place the small circle over it convex side up.

3 Fixing

Use the eyelet tool and a metal mallet to bang the shank down into place. Go gently, and check if it is firmly attached. It is fixed when it stops rattling!

Buying Guide

Make sure you buy the correct-sized eyelet tool at the same time as the metal parts. Ready-packed sets are worth buying if you only need a small number of fittings, because they come with the relevant tools. It is much cheaper to buy eyelets by the hundred however!

Sam Brown studs

Feet

1 Attaching studs

These versatile studs, named after the military belt, are my favourite fittings. They act just like a button, and screw on in two parts. Make a small hole to accommodate the narrow screw part of the shank on the lower surface to be joined, and screw the two parts together. Tighten with a screwdriver if necessary.

2 Making a buttonhole

Measure the size of the top button part of the stud. Make a hole smaller than the circumference of the head, and add a small slit going away from the edge, to create a buttonhole effect.

Feet are used on the base of some leather goods to lift them up from the surface for protection. Solid screw-in case feet can be purchased, but beware of the weight they will add to your project. The two-pronged feet shown here can be inserted through a hole made by an awl. Open up the prongs on the other side, and cover with a circle of glued leather.

In Place

Use feet to hold a piece of stabilizing card or thin plastic in place at the bottom of a bag between the leather and the lining.

Press studs

1 Materials

The thickness of the leather is important to bear in mind when selecting press studs (poppers and domes). Ensure that the shanks are long enough to go through the chosen project. The next task is to separate the four parts and work out which goes with which. A special tool is required to hold the different parts in place during insertion.

2 Assembling female poppers

Select the two parts which make up the 'female' part of the popper: the dome (used on the strap here). Make a hole in the leather and fix the parts in the corresponding two tools. Bang together carefully with a rubber mallet in order not to damage the shape of the metal.

3 Attaching male poppers

Replace the tools with the set for the 'male' popper (the stud) and repeat the process, making sure you put the fittings on the correct sides of the leather.

Magnetic clasp

1 Marking

Mark the positions of the magnetic clasp pieces by drawing a square on the reverse (flesh side) of the leather where they will sit. Glue reinforcing squares on the wrong side of the leather and cut an extra one to glue over the back of each part to protect the leather from rubbing. After marking the position of the closure, press the prongs of the magnet into the leather on the surface to create an indentation. Cut two small slits through the leather and backing, and pass the prongs through.

2 Inserting

Place the washer over the prongs, and press them flat on the reverse side. Glue the second square over the top. Because the metal pierces the top piece, this type of magnet is usually placed in a lining, for example on the flap of a bag. Invisible magnets can also be sourced, which simply glue in behind the leather and do not pierce it.

intermediate
★★

patent belt

This design plays with a plethora of different-sized studs
and rings – select a range of fittings that you like and
adapt the design accordingly. By the time you have
attached them all, you will be an expert!

Materials

Leather: Patent finish cowhide shoulder, or 2.5–3mm thick (6–7oz) belt hide, 0.3–0.4m sq (3–4ft sq). Lambskin or suede for lining (optional)

Tools and equipment:
Scalpel or craft knife
Cutting mat and metal ruler
Scribe or round (scratch) awl
Sand paper
Oval slot punch
Bone folder
Acrylic leather paint
Hand-held rivet setter
Rotary punch, rubber mallet
Leather glue: Impact adhesive, superglue
1 x nickel plated O-ring, 6cm (2⅜in)
20 x nickel plated rivet studs, with long shanks
4 x nickel plated D-rings, 2cm (¾in)
2 x nickel plated O-rings, 5cm (2in)
1 x nickel plated D-ring, 4cm (1½in)
3 x nickel plated Sam Brown studs, with long screw shanks, 1cm (⅜in)

Template: page 150

1 Cut a belt to the desired length, 9cm (3½in) wide, following the template on page 150 for 76–80cm (30–32in) waist. The two rounded belt ends should just meet at the front, so lengthen or shorten the belt to fit the required waist measurement accordingly. Cut out the following pieces:
1 x main belt; 1 x tab A;
1 x strap B; 2 x tab C;
2 x tab D; 1 x tab E;
2 x strap F; 1 x front strap G;
1 x front strap H.
Twelve pieces in total.

2 Scribe the positions of the tabs and straps onto the surface of the belt. Scratch carefully inside the line with a scalpel or piece of sand paper to create a rough surface to hold the glue.

3 If the flesh side of your chosen leather is not smooth, or for sheer luxury, you may decide to line the belt. Simply glue the main shape down to the flesh side of a soft suede or lambskin, make sure all the edges are pressed down and well stuck, and trim carefully around the shape. Machine or hand stitch in place if desired (optional).

4 Punch a slot either side of the centre line of the belt with an oval slot punch, as marked on the template. Glue the two long strips G and H together, and burnish and paint the edges. Burnish and paint the raw edges of all the pieces, including inside the slots, as necessary.

5 Centre back: Attach tab A to the large central O-ring, following the instructions on page 73. Pare the flesh side at one end of the tab, mark and pierce the rivet hole in with a rotary hole punch, and scratch the strap surface to be glued down. Glue the tab in place round the ring, and down to the belt. Make the hole through into the belt and fix in place with a rivet stud (see page 72). Insert strap B through the slots to fix the ring in place, and add one small D-ring at either end of the strap. Attach tabs C to the other side of the D-rings.

6 Front fastenings: Attach tabs D, holding the 5cm (2in) O-rings in place. Attach tab E to the other side of the O-ring on one side only, and attach the large D-ring to the

Hammering it Home

To transfer the holes to the main body of the belt, you will need a hand-held single punch and hammer for areas which you cannot reach with the rotary punch. If you do not have access to this, you can turn the rotary punch over and hammer it onto the hide, but go gently so that you do not damage it.

other side. Position strap F over the top, with a small D-ring attached at the lower end, and rivet down. On the other side, attach the front fastening G and H glued together, by wrapping the single thickness end of G round the ring, and fixing the whole down to the belt. Rivet strap F over, attaching a small D-ring as before.

7 The front fastening of this belt makes use of three Sam Brown studs instead of a buckle. Scratch and glue one end in place on the belt, and attach the Sam Brown studs. The studs should be positioned so that the two ends of the belt just touch.

8 Bend the strap back on itself, mark and pierce the holes and add the 'buttonhole' slits (see page 75). Choose fairly chunky studs with large heads, and do not make the holes for the buttonholes too big, or the studs will rattle around and not hold tight. If the studs will not pass through the hole, make the slit longer and persevere – the leather will be stiff at first.

Stud Selection

Choose the sizes of the rivet studs according to the thickness of the leather through which they must pass – the rivets holding straps F at the front will need to be long enough to go through 3–4 layers of leather. If the head of a rivet sits on top of the leather instead of fitting snugly into the hole, make the hole bigger. For extra strong fixing of studs and rivets, put a tiny drop of superglue on the shank before fixing together. Sam Browns in particular can work loose over time.

intermediate
★★

classic duffel

In a beautiful soft, naturally-coloured leather, this timeless design will age and wear well. Many variations on this pattern can be made: consider altering the proportions, adding zips and flaps to the pockets, or a double row of eyelets around the top.

Materials

Leather: 3 skins of lamb nappa, or a chrome-tanned leather with a waterproof finish, 0.65m sq (7ft sq)
Lining fabric, 1m (1yd)
Plastic or polypropylene sheet, 25cm sq (9¾in sq)
Firm iron-on interfacing, 1m (1yd), iron-on adhesive
5mm (¼in) braided leather cord, 2m (8ft)

Tools and equipment:
Scalpel or craft knife
Cutting mat and metal ruler
Magic pen
Masking tape
Domestic sewing machine, walking foot, leather needle
Polyester thread
Masking tape
Bone folder
Leather glue: Impact adhesive or latex glue
Large round hole punch
Eyelet setting tool (hand-held)
Metal hammer, rubber mallet
12 x brass eyelets, 2.5cm (1in)
2 x brass rivet studs

Template: page 151

1 Draw a pattern following the template on page 151. Measure the skins to check the size – you may have to shrink the pattern slightly if the leather is not large enough. Cut out: 1 x square base; 2 x bag sides; 1 x pocket piece. For the lining, omit the shaded area on the template. Cut the bag wall in one piece: fold the fabric double and place the pattern on the fold (remove the 1cm/⅜in turning). Cut one base square and one pocket lining. Cut a 25cm (4in) square (omitting seam allowance) from plastic or polypropylene sheet to reinforce the base.

2 Apply interfacing up to the line marked on both main body pieces. Iron-on dressmaking interfacing can be used – always do a test piece with a moderate iron and covering cloth to see how the leather responds. Interfacing should be cut to sit just inside the seam allowance, 1cm (⅜in) smaller than the piece of leather. Apply interfacing to the pocket pieces, up to the line indicated, and to the base.

3 Draw in the top fold line on the inside of each of the largest leather pieces. This will be turned over where the eyelets will sit. With a magic pen, mark in the dots for the centre of the eyelet holes, the lines where the pockets will sit, and all other markings indicated on the pattern.

4 Bond the lining fabric to the inside of the pocket pieces up to the fold line, using the iron-on adhesive paper. Fold the top 2cm (¾in) of each pocket over on the line where the interfacing stops, and glue down. Top stitch along the edge. Place the pocket on the main body of leather, hold in place with masking tape, and machine stitch at either side 5mm (¼in) in from the raw edge, to secure the pocket in place within the seam. Work in any loose threads.

5 Place the two body pieces wrong sides together. Machine stitch the side seams together, beginning 1cm (⅜in) in from the edge of the leather at the bottom edge. Bone and glue the seams flat open, work in threads as before, and trim any excess leather along the seams.

6 Cut a slit up to the stitching line on the seam allowance at the base of the bag where two of the corners will sit (see template). Attach the base, leaving the needle in at the corner above the slit, lifting the presser foot, and moving the leather round, so that the four sides sit evenly. You may need to reinforce these corners by stitching round them a second time. Trim the corners of the base at an angle after stitching, and cut away any excess seam allowance. Glue the plastic base square to the leather base of the bag, and turn right side out.

7 Cut out the two lining pieces as indicated on the template. Machine stitch the side seams and overlock or zigzag to prevent fraying. Attach the base as described above, and trim the seam allowance at the bottom. Position the lining inside the bag, matching up the corners and side seams, and bond in place up to the fold line at the top of the bag, using a strip of iron-on adhesive paper around the top. Glue the fold of leather down over the lining on the inside, and press with the bone folder to smooth and flatten the edge. Top stitch the edge if desired.

8 Make the holes for the eyelets (see page 74) as indicated on the pattern. For the best finish, place the eyelet with the long shank on the outside of the bag, so that any imperfections that may arise during the insertion process will be on the inside.

9 Cut a 1.5m (5ft) length of braided cord. Thread the cord through the eyelets with the loose ends coming out at the rear side seam. Place the ends through the eyelet hole at the base of the bag and tie in a double knot inside to secure them. Insert the remaining braid through the eyelet in the central pocket, tying a knot on the outside for decoration.

10 Cut a leather strip 8 x 12cm (3⅛ x 4¾in). Draw a line lengthwise down the centre on the back and glue the sides up to this to create a strip 4 x 12cm (1½ x 4¾in). Wrap the strip round the two plaited cords with an overlap between them, and fix in place with two brass rivet studs. The toggle should be just loose enough to slide along the cords to close the bag.

easy

★

make-up bag

The best quality leathers use the full grain and natural surface of the leather, but many fashion leathers are made from cuts of leather where the top layer has been removed. These are known as 'splits'. Splits are often highly decorated and coated with plastic or cellulose to disguise the nature of the surface. They also have wipe-clean or waterproof properties. You can really have fun with this project by choosing a leather split with a bright, shiny or patterned surface to withstand the rigours of travelling/the party circuit!

Materials

Leather: Lightweight
    patterned fashion or
    chrome-tanned leather with
    a waterproof surface,
    0.2m sq (2ft sq). One skin
    will make 2–3 bags
Waterproof lining, 0.5m (½yd)
Polypropylene or plastic sheet

Tools and equipment:
Card, pencil and metal ruler
Scalpel or craft knife
Cutting mat
Magic pen
Zip, 24cm (9½in)
Masking tape
Domestic sewing machine,
    walking foot, leather needle
Polyester thread
Leather glue: Impact adhesive
Rotary hole punch
Bone folder
Rivet setter
4 x nickel plated feet
8 x small nickel plated rivet
    studs
2 x nickel plated O-rings,
    3.5cm (1½in)
Ordinary hand sewing needle

Template: page 152

1 Make a pattern following the template on page 152. Mark up and cut out one rectangle of leather. Cut the lining as for the leather pattern, but remove the corner areas shaded on the template. Cut a piece of plastic 18 x 9cm (7 x 3½in) for the base of the bag.

2 Draw the fold lines on the inside of the leather with a magic pen, including the zip line with two V shapes at each end. Cut this line into the leather with a scalpel. Turn back the edges and glue in place, making an opening for the zip to sit in.

3 Tape the zip into the slot. Turn over and machine stitch round the outside of the slot close to the edge (see Braided Case, page 130). Remove the tape after stitching.

4 Fold the bag with wrong sides together and the open zip at the top. Machine stitch the side and base seams of the bag, 1cm (⅜in) in from the edge. Trim the corners at an angle and glue the seams flat.

5 Turn the bag right side out and glue the plastic base sheet in place using the fold lines marked inside as a guide. Insert four metal feet into the base through the leather and plastic (see page 75).

6 Fold up the triangle created at each corner of the base, and press into shape with a bone folder. Position the end of the triangle round a ring, and glue and rivet in place. Repeat for the other corner. Alternatively, cut a strip and attach it to the triangle and round the ring.

7 To make up the lining, follow the steps for cutting the zip opening as before, and tack the folded edges in place. Machine stitch the side and base seams together in the same way as for the leather. Trim the corners and seam allowance and press flat.

8 Insert the lining into the bag through the open zip, and hand stitch to the zip with a small neat herringbone stitch.

9 Fold the top corners of leather into triangles, and attach them to the side-rings with glue and rivet studs as in Step 6.

Recycle

Instead of buying new plastic sheet, recycle an old plastic file cover to create this base stabilizer.

key holder

This handy little holder makes a great gift – it really does make life easier on the linings of your pockets, and is very simple to make. The strong contrast between the rich chocolate brown of the thick leather and the zingy orange of the lacing adds a level of sophistication and masculinity to a humble accessory.

Materials

Leather: Offcuts of firm
   leather, 1.5–2mm thick
   (4–5 oz)
Flat 3mm (⅛in) lace in a
   contrasting colour

Tools and equipment:
Scalpel or craft knife
Cutting mat
Metal ruler
Scribe or round (scratch) awl
Oval slot punch
Rubber mallet
Acrylic leather paint
Paintbrush
Leather glue: Impact adhesive
Pronged chisel or lacing fork
Lacing needle (two-prong
   needle)
Lacing nippers (optional)
Glover's needle
Polyester thread
Key ring
Press stud (dome, poppers)
Carnauba cream wax
Cotton cloth

Template: page 150

1 Following the template on page 150, cut out two pieces for the holder and two strap pieces, 1 x 18.5cm (7¼in) long; 1 x 17.5cm (6¾in) long.

2 Cut a slot with an oval slot punch where shown on the template on one body piece.

3 Glue the two strap pieces together and paint the edges. Paint all the raw edges including the slot if desired – even though they will be laced over on the main body of the holder, they will still show through the gaps.

4 Lightly glue the very edges of the two body parts together, and then prepare the edges for lacing as shown in the Braided Case project (see page 132). Pierce the lacing holes approx. 3mm (⅛in) in from the edge with a flat pronged chisel (lacing fork).

5 Wax and soften the lace (see page 130). If you prefer, you can experiment with ribbon as an alternative, as in the key holder illustrated. (If you use ribbon, wax and polish the leather first, as it will mark the ribbon if you do it afterwards.) Thread the lacing needle, and glue the end of the lace between the two layers of leather.

6 Whipstitch round the edges of the key holder. Whipstitch is achieved by an oversewing motion, bringing the lace through a pair of holes, over the edge of the leather and back through the next pair.

7 Attach the flat end of the strap to the key ring: pare the end, glue it round the ring, and hand stitch it in place. Pull the strap through the slot from the inside, so that the key ring sits inside.

8 Check that the press stud is appropriate for the thickness of the leather you are using. Insert the two parts of the press stud as shown on page 76. Place the 'female' part on the body of the key holder on the opposite side to the slot, and the 'male' on the end of the strap.

9 When the press stud is done up, the keys should sit snugly within the holder. Undoing the press stud will allow them to slip out of the holder to be used. Polish the key holder with carnauba cream and a soft cloth.

Variations

This design is also very effective if saddle stitched together, instead of laced. Vary the design by using russet leather and stamping decoration as illustrated on page 107, or try it with an edge of Mexican braid, as shown for the Braided Case on page 132.

decorative

This chapter only scratches the surface of the possibilities for adding decorative detail to your design projects. I have tried to include methods that can be adapted for a wide variety of objects – the cufflink knots can make great bag fastenings, key rings and even necklaces, made in different sizes and colours, and the stamped or embossed effect on the compact case can be applied to any number of projects, from bookmarks to belts and bag straps.

Monkey's Fist Knot

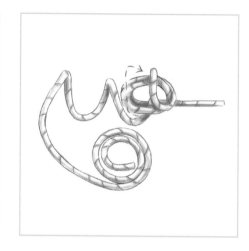

1 **Coiling**
Coil the lace three times round your first and second finger to make three even loops.

2 **Turning**
Hold the coils together between finger and thumb and turn them 90 degrees.

3 **Wrapping**
Begin to wrap the lace round the coils in the direction shown in the diagram.

decorative

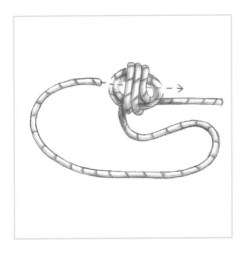

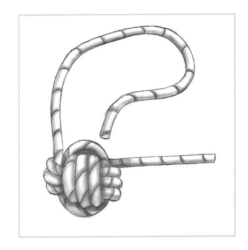

4 Threading through

When you have made three more coils, turn the knot and bring the end of the lace through the centre of the knot in the direction shown.

5 Second wrap

Wrap the lace round the second set of coils as indicated in the diagram.

6 Third coil

Repeat Step 5 to make a second coil. Make a third coil in the same way.

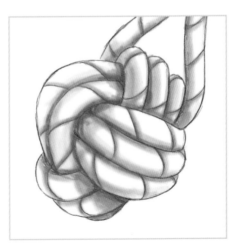

7 Pulling thread

Bring the lace through the centre of the knot once more and out near the other loose end.

8 Tightening

Work through the entire knot, pulling the coils tight, until it looks like the diagram.

Stamping

Hot Stuff

This technique for wet stamping is suitable for vegetable-tanned leather only. Chrome-tanned leather may be stamped and embossed, but it requires the application of heat. Hot foil and embossing machines are available, and book binders may emboss logos, monograms and other designs for you.

1 Dampening

Lightly dampen russet leather by running it briefly under the cold tap, or immersing in a bowl of water. Let the moisture sink into the leather for a couple of minutes.

2 Impressing

A wide variety of hand-stamps can be found; successful designs are often built up using a limited range of three or four shapes repeated in different combinations. Use the rubber mallet to impress the stamp into the surface of the leather and leave to dry – the slight variation in pressure between each impression adds a feeling of vitality to the pattern.

Dyeing

1 Applying even coats

When dyeing leather, always wear latex gloves and apply in a well-ventilated area. This dye can be hard to remove from stained fingers (try nail polish remover or thinners if required). Apply even coats of dye to dry leather with a large brush or sponge. Dark colours are easier to achieve, because it takes practice to apply the dye evenly. Colour can be diluted with cellulose thinners. Ensure you have an extractor mask and good ventilation if you are going to do this regularly.

2 Polishing

Let the dye sink in for 10–15 minutes, then polish the surface with a clean dry cloth to remove excess pigment, and seal and wax the surface with a coat of saddle soap followed by a paint-on leather varnish.

Punching

1 Transferring design

A very simple way of adding pattern to leatherwork is to pierce holes on one layer and back it with a piece in a contrasting colour or texture. Transfer your design to the back of the top leather with a magic pen. If the design is symmetrical, it can be folded in half so that both sides are punched at once.

2 Piercing holes

Punch out the holes with a rotary hole punch and/or a single punch as required. Experiment with different sizes of holes to bring variety into the design.

3 Applying glue

Apply glue carefully to the back of the leather so that it will not be seen through the holes, and glue the contrasting piece face down to the back.

easy

★

knotty cufflinks

The intricacy of a leather knot can be a great contrast against a plain cotton shirt. This technique can also be used to make a very good key fob, button or bag accessory. To make the knot larger, simply use a thicker lace or cord to tie it in. Try a round lace, or even two contrasting laces together – this takes a lot of patience, as it is very hard to get the two colours to lie evenly together but the effect is worth it!

Materials

Leather: Small scraps of firm
leather, approx. 2mm thick
(5oz), and thinner pieces of
a toning colour
Flat thonging lace 3mm (⅛in)
wide, 1m (1yd)

Tools and equipment:
Scalpel or craft knife
Cutting mat
Metal ruler
Carnauba cream wax
Cotton cloth
Scribe or round (scratch) awl
Leather glue: Impact adhesive
Large round punch set
Rotary hole punch
Rubber mallet
Acrylic leather paint
Paintbrush

1 Cut a 30cm (1ft) length of flat lace for each cufflink. Soften the lacing by pulling it through a cloth covered with carnauba wax several times. Polish away any surplus wax.

2 Follow the steps for the Monkey's Fist knot (see pages 96–97), leaving a good length of lace at either end for tying the knot. Use the end of a scribe to pull the loops tight one by one after tying, and to push the strands into their correct place when tidying the look of the knot.

3 Find some offcuts of a thin leather that tones with the colour of the lace. Glue it onto some firm belt leather or russet. Choose a large round punch with a circle approx. 1.5cm (½in) diameter. Check that the circle will fit through the cuff buttonholes before going any further! Punch out four circles from the underside of the leather. Make a hole with an ordinary rotary hole punch in the centre of two of the circles.

4 Trim the two ends of lace coming out of the knot down to 4cm (1½in) in length. Glue the 1.5cm (½in) nearest the knot together to create a stalk. Pass the remaining two ends through the hole in one of the circles, with the coloured side topmost. Pare, trim and glue the lace to the underside of this circle. Glue the remaining circle on top, with the coloured leather facing outward, so that the lace ends are sandwiched between the two circles and cannot be seen.

5 Paint the raw sides of the circles if desired, with acrylic leather paint to match.

Keeping Lace in Place

When winding the lace, always keep the coloured side facing outward – it can easily get twisted, and this will spoil the look of the finished knot.

intermediate
★★

cherry compact

This design was influenced by Chinese carved boxes, and uses stamped patterns, a rich cherry-red dye and coloured wax to create an antique feel. Stamped designs on leather are very versatile – you can use them effectively for a contemporary look, too.

Materials

Leather: Vegetable-tanned
   hide (russet), 0.1m sq
   (1ft sq), 2–2.5mm thick
   (5–6oz)
Round plastic or glass
   compact mirror, approx.
   7.5cm (3in) diameter

Tools and equipment:
Pair of compasses and card
Scalpel or craft knife
Cutting mat
Leather glue: Impact
   adhesive, latex glue, PVA
Bone folder
Edge-creaser
Scribe or round awl
Stamping tools
Bulldog clips
Stitching awl
Pricking wheel
Cork block
2 x harness needles, size 4
Waxed linen thread
Latex gloves
Red leather dye
2 x paintbrushes
Carnauba cream wax, cloth
Leather varnish (Tan Kote)
Antique wax or dark shoe
   polish

1 Measure the diameter of the compact mirror. Mark up two circles of leather 5mm (¼in) larger than the radius of the mirror. Cut a smaller circle inside one of them, 1.5cm (½in) smaller in radius than the outer measurement. When marking up the first circle, place the point of the compasses on a piece of card to protect the leather. This is not necessary for the second one as it will be cut away, and is useful to mark the centre to ensure that the inside circle is drawn from the same point.

2 Cut out the circles very carefully, trying to keep the blade upright and the shape intact. Measure and mark the centre on the inside of the first circle and draw a line to the radius of the mirror as a guide. Glue the mirror face up in the centre. Glue the cut out circle on top with impact adhesive. Press down the edges with a bone folder, creating a clear line round the edge of the mirror. Edge-crease this outer lip if desired (see page 16).

3 Cut two more circles, 1.5cm (½in) larger in radius than the new measurement of the encased mirror. Cut a small round dip from each circle, to allow the mirror to be pulled out of the case.

4 Use an edge-creaser to mark a line 3mm (⅛in) in from the edge, around both larger circles. Create a stamped design to sit within this line (see page 98). The design should leave a space of at least 1cm (⅜in) around the outer edge for stitching. Practise the design (and circle cutting) on some spare pieces first, and then impress it onto both of the circles. Leave the leather to dry and the pattern to set overnight, or for a few hours in a warm dry environment.

5 Hold the case together with bulldog clips, and check that you only stitch up to the point where you can remove and replace the mirror. Adjust as required. Lightly glue the edges of the outer case together with latex glue or PVA, up to these points.

6 Mark and pierce the stitching holes along the creased line up to the points previously marked. Use a stitching or pricking wheel, awl and cork block as described on pages 42–43. Stitch the two pieces together with linen thread, using saddle stitch (see page 45).

7 Protect your hands with latex gloves, and follow the steps for dyeing on page 99. Do not apply the dye until the leather is thoroughly dry, or it will not penetrate evenly. Remove excess dye with a clean cloth and small amount of carnauba cream. Burnish the inside and outside edges of the mirror thoroughly to compress and seal them before applying the wax and varnish to seal the dye.

8 Apply a black or dark brown antique wax to the outer case, following the steps on page 99. Let this wax dry in thoroughly and polish off several times before giving it a final sealing coat of varnish.

Mirror, Mirror

Source a small round plastic or glass compact mirror. Liberate one from an old compact, or ask a glass merchant to cut some from thin glass or plastic sheet.

advanced

moroccan slippers

A pair of made-to-measure slippers is a hard gift to beat. With a simple pattern of pierced holes and luxurious metallic backing leather, these Moroccan-style slippers are almost elegant enough to wear outdoors!

Materials

Leather: Suede skin 0.55m sq (5–6ft sq); metallic chrome-tanned leather, 0.2m sq (2ft sq); cowhide or russet shoulder, 45cm sq (17¾in sq), 4mm (10oz) thick

Tools and equipment:
Card, pencil and ruler
Rotary hole punch, single hole punch, rubber mallet
Magic pen
Scalpel or craft knife
Cutting mat
Leather glue: Impact adhesive
Domestic sewing machine, walking foot, leather needle
Polyester thread
Scribe or round (scratch) awl
Bone folder
French curves or curved ruler
Stitching awl
Pricking iron (stitching fork)
Pricking wheel
2 x harness needles, size 4
Waxed linen thread
Glover's needle
Carnauba cream wax, cloth
Acrylic leather paint
Paintbrush

Template: page 148

1 Draw round the sole of your foot or an existing pair of soft shoes. Transfer the shape to card, and adapt to create a sole shape you like, adding 5mm (¼in) around the outside (see page 56).

2 Create a card pattern for the upper, based on the template on page 148. Adapt it to fit your sole size and shape. The measurement around the toe from point A to B on the sole should match the measurement of the round edge of the upper.

3 Draw a design for a punched pattern onto your card template, using different-sized holes if you desire. Punch the holes into the card, and lay the card onto the flesh side of the top suede. Draw round the shape, and transfer the punched design through the holes with a magic pen. Turn the pattern over and repeat for the other foot.

4 Cut out the leather to be punched. Cut out two further pieces of top leather for the inner lining, and then cut two metallic lining pieces from the same pattern, but without the 1cm (⅜in) seam allowance at the top.

5 Punch out the patterns in the top leathers using a rotary hole punch. Remember to keep a firm piece of leather backing behind the top leather to punch into (see page 14).

6 Apply small points of glue to the wrong side of the suede between the punched patterns and press the metallic leather in place quickly, leaving the 1cm (⅜in) turning at the top edge of the suede. Place the lining suede on top of the punched piece right sides together, and machine stitch along the top edge. Trim the seam, turn right side out, and roll the edge to create a neat finish. Apply an even layer of glue to the back of the metallic leather, and press the lining suede quickly into place.

Making an Impact

Impact adhesive is usually applied to both surfaces and allowed to dry, but here it is used on one side only and pieces are pressed together when the glue is still wet.

7 Cut two soles for each foot from firm cowhide or russet. Burnish the surface with a cloth and the sides with a bone folder. Cut a heel shape for each foot (see page 56). Scratch the leather surface, and glue the heels to the grain side of the sole for each foot.

8 Draw a line round the curve of the top leather on the inside, 5mm (¼in) in from the edge. Scratch a corresponding line 5mm (¼in) around the edge of the remaining sole pieces without heels, between points A and B. Glue the pieces together. For a neat edge, glue the top leather very slightly over the sole edge, and then trim with a sharp blade. Using waxed linen thread, hand stitch the upper to the sole along the 5mm (¼in) glue line. Repeat for the other slipper. (You may be able to do this on the machine with a large stitch.)

9 Glue the heel and sole pieces to the stitched uppers. Burnish the edges to a smooth shine, and wax if desired. The edges of the slippers in the image have been painted with acrylic edge paint to match the colour of the uppers.

Quick Step

You could purchase ready-cut leather soles from a shoemaker instead of cutting your own.

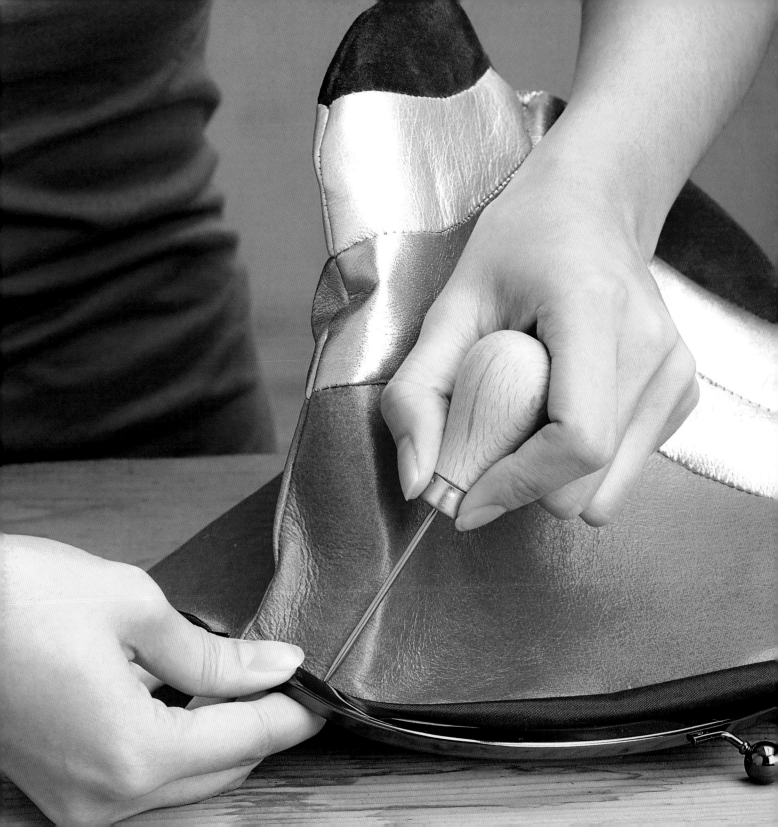

advanced techniques

The projects in this chapter are not difficult in themselves, but they are challenging because they require a degree of perseverance, planning and refinement, and combine different techniques to take you to the next stage. Having experimented with and mastered some of the techniques covered so far, you will enjoy putting them together to make a substantial article to be proud of – the Record Bag combines stitching and metal fittings, but also involves the use of interfacings and lining, and the Deco Bag gives you a chance to create your own unique pattern. You will soon be designing your own leatherwork pieces with ease.

advanced
★★★

record bag

This advanced project is a contemporary take on the classic satchel. It is best made in a supple, textured cow hide, which may not be suitable for every domestic machine. An alternative is to choose a lighter weight skin, and back it with very firm interfacing or canvas.

Materials

Leather: Side of medium weight cow
 hide, 1.6–2mm thick (4–5oz)
Firm iron-on interfacing, 1m (1yd)
Lining fabric, 1m (1yd)

Tools and equipment:
Scalpel or craft knife
Cutting mat
Long metal ruler
Scribe or round (scratch) awl
Magic pen
Leather glue: Impact adhesive
Acrylic leather paint
Paintbrush
Sand paper
Glover's needle
Polyester thread
Oval slot punch and rubber or metal
 mallet
2 x single nickel plated buckles, 2cm
 (¾in)
Small nickel plated rivet studs
Hand-held rivet setter
Domestic sewing machine, walking
 foot, leather needle
Bulldog clips
Bone folder
Rotary punch
2 x nickel plated square rings, 4cm
 (1½in)
1 x nickel plated double slide, 4cm
 (1½in)

Template: page 153

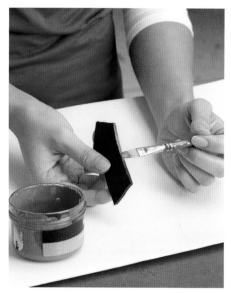

1 Cutting pattern pieces

Cut out all the pattern pieces
following the template on page 153. Cut
one main body piece, one gusset and one
strap. Cut two of the front panel shape (one
of the flap lining), and two buckle holder
tabs. Cut four buckle straps, four buckle
plackets and four side plackets. Apply iron-
on interfacing to the gusset, two front panel
shapes and main body piece of the bag,
inside the 1cm (⅜in) seam allowance.

2 Gluing double pieces

Glue two side placket pieces together
for each side of the bag, to give the square
rings holding the strap more strength. Glue
two buckle strap pieces double, and two
buckle plackets double in the same way.
Paint the edges of all these double pieces
in a contrasting coloured acrylic leather
paint to match the stitching thread chosen.

3 Attaching plackets

Scratch the surface of the leather with a scalpel or sand paper at each point on the gusset where the side plackets will be attached. Glue the plackets in place, and stitch firmly to the leather by hand with a Glover's needle and contrasting thread.

4 Punching slots

Punch a slot in each buckle holder tab with a slot punch and rubber mallet. If your leather is thick, you may need to use a heavier metal mallet for this. Test that the hole is big enough to allow the tongue of the buckle to rotate fully. If not, lengthen as required.

5 Finishing buckle tab

Pare the end of the buckle holder tab, insert the buckle and glue the tab back onto itself, to hold the buckle in place. Glue and rivet stud the buckle holder tab to the buckle placket. Scratch the front of the bag where marked on the template, and glue and stitch the whole piece in place. Repeat for the other buckle.

6 Machine stitching

Pare or skive the edges of the main body piece, gusset, front panel and flap lining pieces. Place the leather flap lining piece onto the main body piece right sides together. Machine stitch round the outside edge allowing 1cm (⅜in) turning. Clip the curved seams in a series of small V shapes.

7 Attaching gusset

Attach the gusset piece to the other end of the main body piece. Hold the pieces together with bulldog clips and machine stitch. Clip the seams.

8 Rolling seams

Attach the front of the bag, then trim the seams to 5mm (¼in) width, turn the bag right side out and roll the edges so that the shape is clear and any small creases are removed. Cut out and sew up three lining pieces following the template on page 153. Clip the seams as before but do not trim. Press the seams flat open with a cool iron. Insert the lining into the bag, glue it lightly in place under the leather flap lining at the back of the bag. Turn 1cm (⅜in) of the raw edge at the top of the front and sides of the bag over the lining, hold in place with bulldog clips, and glue down lightly. Top stitch round the edge and across the flap lining where it covers the bag lining, to hold the lining in place.

All in One

A side of cow hide is between 1.8–2.5m sq (20–25ft sq). This is enough to make four or more bags, and allows the strap to be cut in a single length. This hide will need to be pared or skived at the edges if you wish to sew it on a domestic machine. You could choose a lighter weight skin as long as it is not too stretchy, and apply a firm interfacing or canvas. Smaller skins mean that it will not be possible to cut the strap in one piece. Webbing is a good strong alternative.

9 Cutting strap

Glue the strap piece down to the uncut leather remnant, flesh sides together. Glue it as straight as possible, by lining one edge up against a long straight ruler. Cut along the straight edges of the strap so that you have a strap of double thickness. It is more accurate to glue the leather first than to try to glue two long strips together after they have been cut. Cut the second strip 5cm (2in) longer than the first at each end. Paint the edges, if desired.

10 Attaching slide

Pare one of the single ends of the longer strap, and glue it in place round the central bar of the slide. Peel up the end of the strap lining, tuck the pared end underneath, and glue the strap down again. Stitch firmly together.

11 Finishing

Loop the strap through one of the side rings on the gusset of the bag from the back. Bring the end back through both openings in the slide as shown. Attach the end to the other side of the bag, and stitch firmly to secure. Finally, attach the buckle straps. Stitch to the underside of the front flap where marked. Place through the buckle to mark the position of the hole, and punch three holes in the strap.

advanced
★★★

moulded bowl

The art of moulding leather to make vessels and containers is very old indeed – there is a fabulous collection of blackjacks or old leather bottles at the British Museum – and it was also used to make armour, buckets and shields. The term 'cuir bouilli' is sometimes used to describe moulded leather items. This fascinating process permanently fixed three-dimensional shapes into leather, by a combination of hot water, pressure and possibly even boiling wax. The leather tray in this project is a much simpler process, but follows in the same tradition.

Materials

Leather: Vegetable-tanned hide
    (russet), 1.5–2.5mm thick (4–6oz)
    (size depends on mould)

Tools and equipment:
Plaster of Paris, plaster polymer
    (optional)
Scalpel or craft knife
Cutting mat
Metal ruler
Mould, bowl of warm water, washing-
    up liquid
Piece of wooden board, or MDF, to
    staple in to
Staple gun and staples, 6–8mm
    (approx. ¼in) or larger
Bone folder
Cotton cloth
Screwdriver
Latex gloves
Leather dye
Paintbrush
Carnauba cream wax
Acrylic leather paint (optional)

1 Preparation

Measure the length and width of your mould (see Mould Making, opposite) and add 2cm (¾in) extra all round. The leather will stretch when wet, but you need a good margin for stapling down. Cut a piece of russet to the dimensions required, and wet it thoroughly in a bowl of warm water with some washing-up liquid.

2 Softening

Massage the leather thoroughly to soften it, making sure the water has penetrated fully through the layer to the back. Work the leather in your hands until you feel the texture change and become rubbery.

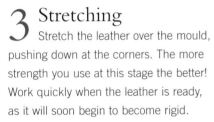

3 Stretching

Stretch the leather over the mould, pushing down at the corners. The more strength you use at this stage the better! Work quickly when the leather is ready, as it will soon begin to become rigid.

4 Stapling

Staple one corner of the leather down to a thick wooden board. Staple as close as possible to the mould. Pull hard on the opposite corner to create a diagonal stretch and staple this down, too. If your staples keep coming out, you may need to use longer ones. Fix down the opposite corners in the same way, keeping the leather tight and flat, and avoiding making pleats at the corners.

Mould Making

The leather in this project is stretched over a former or mould, so the first step is to find, or make and prepare, this mould. Choose a simple shape with no indentations or undercuts, and sloping sides rather than straight ones. I often cast shapes from found objects in plaster of Paris mixed with a waterproof polymer. Cover the surface of the mould with clingfilm if there is any chance that it might stain the leather. Wood is an ideal material for mould making, being strong and flexible, so a turned wooden bowl or shape cut out from MDF will work well. A rigid plastic bowl will also do. Avoid metal, because this will react badly with the russet leather and create a stain.

5 Stapling sides

Work round the mould by stapling the opposite sides in turn, always pulling hard to stretch the leather as taut as possible. This gives strength to the finished shape.

6 Shaping

Use the bone folder to press out any creases that form as the staples get closer together. The leather can be compressed in places, so the moulding process is a mixture of stretching and condensing. Work round the base close to the mould with the bone folder, to delineate the shape as sharply as possible. When the leather is fully stretched, work over the surface with a cotton cloth to burnish it, compress it further and remove excess water. The mould should now be left to dry fully overnight, preferably in a warm place.

7 Cutting free

Cut the leather free from the staples as close to the base as possible. Use a screwdriver to prise the staples up if necessary. Remove the mould and leather from the board and place on a flat smooth surface.

8 Trimming edges

To trim an even edge onto the bowl, find a flat surface such as a thin booklet or cork block to rest the knife on. Score a line round the leather, moving the mould as necessary. Cut along the line, and remove the mould.

9 Dyeing

If you would like to colour the tray, apply the dye evenly to the leather when it is completely dry with a flat paintbrush. (This tray is NOT suitable for use with food!) See the instructions on page 99 for more details on dyeing leather.

10 Finishing

Wax, seal and polish the leather, applying several coats. Burnish the cut edge with a cotton cloth and bone folder, or paint with acrylic paint if desired. The tray will hold its shape as long as it is kept dry – and makes a great desk tidy or calling card receptacle.

advanced

★★★

braided case

Braiding is another decorative technique borrowed from the world of horses and saddlery. Mexican gauchos were famous for the highly skilled workmanship on their tack, and this round braid is named after them. Here, in a rich red, it adds a touch of understated luxury and style to this small, zipped case – perfect for pens, make-up or travelling.

Materials

Leather: Firm cow hide, 0.2m sq
  (2ft sq), 1.5–2mm thick (4–5oz)
Flat lace 3mm (⅛in) wide in a
  contrasting colour, 7.5m (25ft)

Tools and equipment:
Scalpel or craft knife
Cutting mat
Metal ruler
Masking tape
Cotton zip (metal teeth), 23cm (9in)
Domestic sewing machine, Teflon-
  coated zipper foot, leather needle
Polyester thread
Leather glue: Impact adhesive
Lacing fork
4 x lacing needles (two-prong
  needle)
Single lacing chisel or pair of lacing
  nippers (optional)
Scribe or round (scratch) awl
Magic pen
Edge-creaser
Rubber mallet
2 x harness needles, size 4
Pliers
Carnauba cream wax
Cotton cloth

Template: page 153

1 Preparing zip

Cut out the pattern following the template on page 153. Cut the rectangular opening for the zip onto the top piece, and tape the zip in place behind, keeping the masking tape away from the stitching line.

2 Stitching zip

Machine stitch round the zip opening as close to the raw edge as possible. Use a Teflon-coated zipper foot, or hand stitch in place as an alternative.

Softly, Softly

Soften the lace with wax by pulling it through a waxed cloth several times. Stretching the lace in this way helps to make it more pliable and easier to work with. Very firm lace can be drawn across the corner of a table to help soften and stretch it.

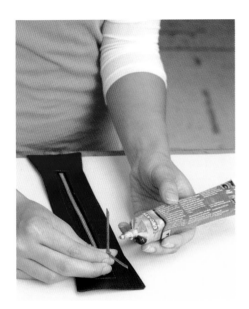

3 Attaching zip pull

Glue a small strip of leather or a scrap of the flat lace used for the braiding onto the end of the zip pull, if desired.

4 Preparing edges

Prepare the edges of both pieces for lacing using a lacing fork with large flat teeth. A single lacing chisel or pair of lacing nippers will also be useful for piercing the curves, but a stitch awl will work in an emergency! The lacing joins the placket to the main piece.

5 Cutting lace

Make sure the flat lace chosen is small enough to fit through the lacing holes easily. Measure out the amount of lace required for the project. Mexican braid requires nine times the length of the area to be laced, so cut this into manageable, arm-sized lengths to make lacing possible.

Gentle Persuasion

Keep a pair of pliers handy for pulling the needle through when it gets stubborn!

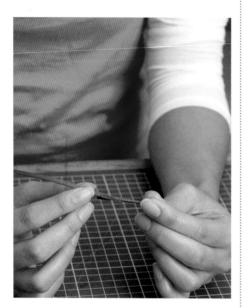

Round Braid or Mexican Braid

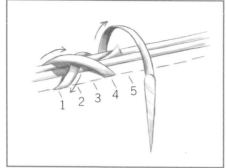

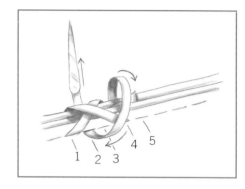

1 First diagonals

Bring the needle out through the third hole on the back, over the top edge and in through both first holes. Bring the needle over the top again and through the fourth holes.

2 Second stage

Bring the lace over the top again, and through the second set of holes.

6 Threading the lace

Pare, or shave, the end of the lace at an angle before inserting it into the lacing needle. The hooks in the needle help to hold the lace in place, but in my experience, you may need two or three needles for one project, as they 'tire' quickly. Glue 1cm (⅜in) of the end of the lace between the two layers of leather at around the second and third holes. Leave a small length of lace and cover it over with the braid as you go along. Braid the two pieces together following the diagrams.

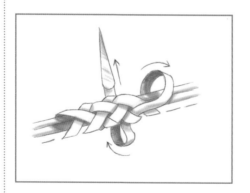

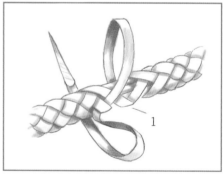

6 Repeating pattern

Weave the needle back over the first diagonal, under the second and through the fourth holes. Each set of holes is laced through twice. Continue the pattern: weave under one diagonal, over one diagonal, forward three sets of holes, over one diagonal, under one diagonal, back two sets of holes.

7 Back to the start

When you have worked round to the starting point, bring the needle through the first set of holes, over the top, over the first diagonal of lace, under the second and back through the last set of holes.

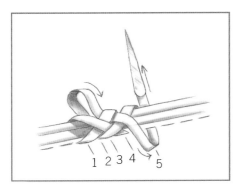

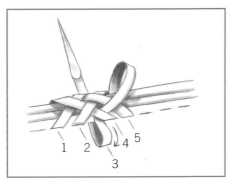

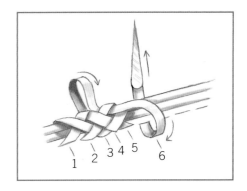

3 Weaving forward
Weave the needle under the first diagonal of lace, over the second and through the fifth set of holes.

4 Weaving back
Bring the lace over the top, and weave the needle back over the first diagonal of lace, under the second and through the third set of holes.

5 Continuing to weave
Weave the lace as before, under the first diagonal of lace, over the second and through the sixth set of holes. Bring the lace over the top.

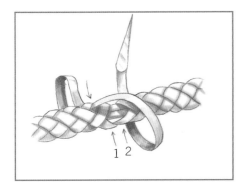

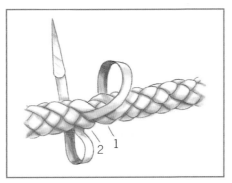

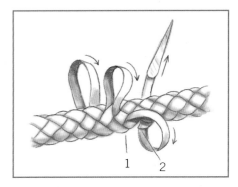

8 Weaving a second layer
Weave the lace as before, under the first diagonal of lace, over the second, bring to the front and go through the second pair of holes.

9 Working back
Bring the lace over the top, and weave the needle back under one diagonal and through the last set of holes.

10 Finishing
Continue in sequence: under the first diagonal, over the next, under the next, and through the front third hole only. Bring the needle out through the lace and cut off close, or bring the needle out inside the case and cut off, leaving a 1cm (⅜in) end to glue to the inside of the seam.

advanced
★★★

deco bag

The process of making this evening bag or purse is very rewarding, building up to the drama of clamping the frame. The decorative curved panels offer great scope for decoration and design – try the same pattern in three colourways and see how different they appear. For added glamour, include at least one metallic leather in your design.

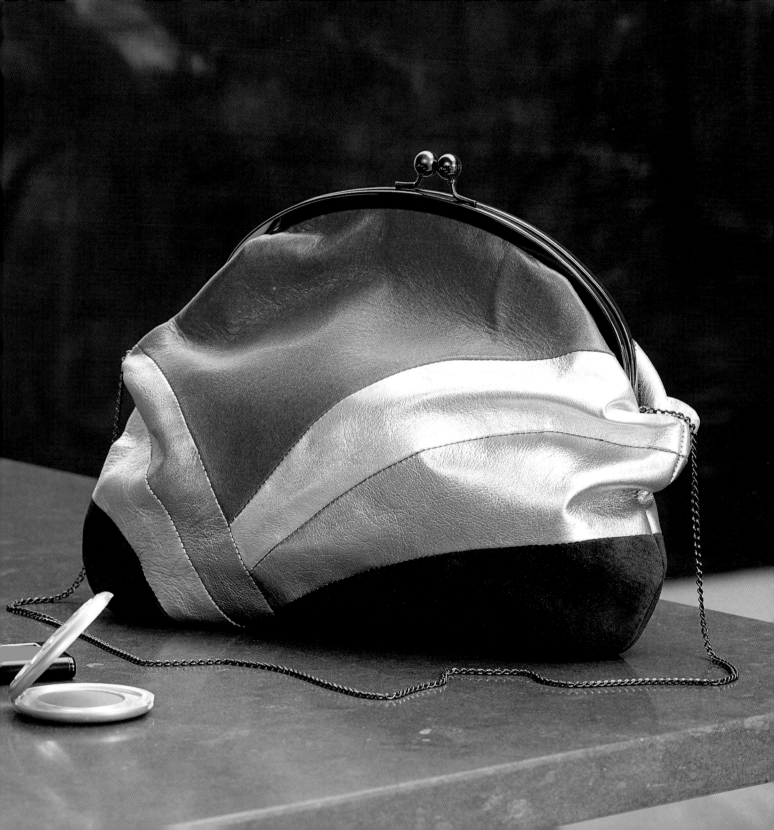

Materials

Leather: Three contrasting colours or
    textures of chrome-tanned lamb
    nappa or suede, including one
    metallic, 0.2m sq (2ft sq) each
Lightweight iron-on interfacing,
    0.5m (½yd)
Acetate or silk lining fabric,
    0.5m (½yd)

Tools and equipment:
Tape measure
Paper or card, pencil and metal ruler
Tracing paper
Scalpel or craft knife
Cutting mat
Magic pen
Bone folder
French curves or curved ruler
Glover's or leather needle
Polyester thread
Bulldog clips
Ordinary hand sewing needle
Card spreaders
Leather glue: Impact adhesive or
    rubber cement
Domestic sewing machine, walking
    or Teflon foot, leather needle
Scissors
Metal bag or purse frame,
    20–25.5cm (8–10in)
Round (scratch) awl
Bench vice
Metal chain, 1m (1yd)
Pliers

Template: page 152

1 Cutting pattern pieces

Measure the entire length of your frame opening and adapt the template on page 152 to create a U-shaped paper pattern that fits the frame, allowing 1cm (⅜in) seam allowance. Cut two pieces this shape for the lining. Trace the design onto this shape, and make the pattern pieces by numbering each separate section of the pattern. Add registration (notch) marks to each seam line. Cut out each piece, lay it on a new piece of paper, and draw round it, transferring the notch marks and adding a 1cm (⅜in) seam allowance to each edge. Cut out two of each leather pattern piece, remembering to reverse the pattern for one side, so that the front and back match. Back each piece with iron-on interfacing up to the seam allowance.

2 Clipping curves

Clip the curved areas of each seam allowance inside the 1cm (⅜in) line, to make it easier to fit the curves together when stitching.

3 Stitching

Sew the pattern pieces together in sequence, 1cm (⅜in) in from the edge. Make sure the edges are together at all times, and the notches matched. Manipulate the leather, but do not stretch it! Try not to veer off the stitching line – this is the difficult part. Use bulldog clips to hold the work together. Work in any thread ends with a needle.

4 Gluing seams

Using a card spreader, glue the curved seams flat at the back of the work as shown, running a bone folder along the seam to eliminate any bumps and removing excess leather where necessary. When the two panels have been assembled and glued, machine stitch them together round the curve.

5 Lining

Clip the curves, and trim the seam allowance back to 5mm (¼in). Turn the bag right side out and roll the seam between your fingers to make a neat edge. Sew the lining together, but leave a gap in the seam as marked on the template. The gap should be large enough for the entire leather bag to fit through. (It may be simpler to do this first, before you set the machine up for working on leather.)

Practice Makes Perfect

It is worth practising sewing a few curved seams before you sew the actual bag as they can be tricky!

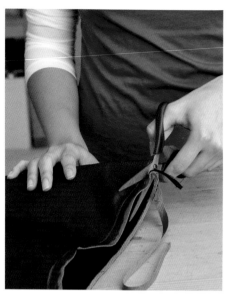

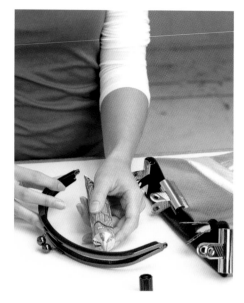

6 Stitching together

Slip the bag inside the lining so that right sides are together. Align the top edges, hold together with bulldog clips if necessary, and stitch all the way round the top of the bag, 1cm (⅜in) in from the edge.

7 Bagging out

Trim the two layers along the seam back to 5mm (¼in). Pull the bag out through the gap in the lining, and push the lining inside the bag, rolling the top seam as before. This is the process known as bagging out.

8 Gluing edges

Press the top edge with a cool iron if desired, or hold together with bulldog clips. Apply a thin film of impact adhesive to the top edge, hold together with bulldog clips, and another inside the frame. There must be enough glue to hold the leather inside the frame, but try to keep the glue line thin, so it will not show outside the width of the frame metal. Ensure that the inside of the frame is fully coated with a thin film of glue right to the edge, by using a small piece of card as a spreader.

Sleeker Fit

To make a sleeker frame bag or purse, curve the outer edges of your pattern down, following the shape of the frame. This will remove the fullness which covers the hinges at the sides. To make a fuller frame bag or purse, use the U-shaped pattern as before for the lining, but make a wider one for the outer leather, adding 10cm (4in) to the top measurement. Gather the fullness into small pleats before attaching to the lining.

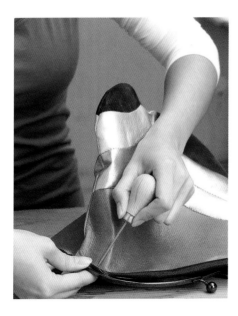

9 Attaching frame

Beginning at one corner, push the leather into the frame as far as it will go, using a round awl with a long blade. Work round the frame eliminating any pleats, and lining up the seams with the frame hinges.

10 Clamping

Protect the frame from the jaws of the bench vice with a towel. Place the frame between the jaws and tighten them steadily, until the frame has closed around the leather completely. A large frame will need to be clamped in sections, so try to keep the pressure even or you may dent the frame.

11 Finishing

Pull the lining back out of the bag, and sew up the hole by hand with a hemming stitch. This could be done before the glue is applied, but you will be far too eager to see the finished bag to want to do it then! Add a length of chain for the strap. Some frame bags are made with small rings already attached, so that it is easy to add a chain, handle or thin leather strap. If your frame does not have this, a ring can be sewn directly onto the leather, concealed within the fold at the side of the bag.

advanced
★★★

vine corsage

Lovely three-dimensional shapes can be achieved by hand moulding vegetable-tanned leather. Dye russet leather after moulding to add colour, or invest in some wonderful Harmatan goatskin, such as that used for the Origami Box, on page 36. Try the technique with flower shapes, rivet and stitch layers together or use two toning colours – the scope is limitless.

Materials

Leather: Small pieces or offcuts of
  vegetable-tanned hide (russet or
  goatskin), 1–1.5mm thick (2–3oz)
Natural coloured round leather lace,
  2mm (¹⁄₁₆in) wide, 30cm (1ft)

Tools and equipment:
Card, pencil and metal ruler
Scalpel or craft knife
Cutting mat
Scribe
Safety beveller or paring knife
Spoon and ball modelling tools
  (optional)
Carnauba cream wax or leather
  varnish
Cotton cloth
Leather glue: PVA and superglue
Silver brooch back

Template: page 150

1 Scribing

To create your leaf pattern, draw
round a real leaf, design a shape from
your imagination or copy the template on
page 150. Leaves with indented edges and
interesting shapes, such as oak, vine and
mulberry, work best, because they give
more scope for working in three-dimensions.
Scribe the pattern onto an offcut of
vegetable-tanned leather.

2 Shaping edges

Cut out the general shape, and then
work round the edges adding the details
using a number of V-shaped cuts. Repeat
to make a second leaf.

3 Paring

As the work is small scale, it is a good idea to pare or skive the back edges of the brooch with a safety beveller, paring knife or scalpel blade. This makes the results much more elegant, and the edges much easier to shape and curl.

4 Softening

Place the leaf in a bowl of luke-warm water, massaging it so that the water penetrates thoroughly. Press on a dry cloth to remove excess moisture. Rub the wet leather between both palms, until you can feel the fibres become rubbery. Let it rest for two or three minutes: the damp leather will be ready to work when you feel it become firmer and less floppy.

5 Moulding

Mould the shape in your hands, by pulling and stretching. The more tension you put on the fibres within the leather, the more they will hold the 3-D shape. Try compressing some areas together, and rolling the edges outward. The heat of your hands will help to set the shape as you work.

6 Adding details

Once the shape is formed, add detail by incising lines or patterns with a scribe. Ball and spoon-shaped leather modelling tools can also be used. Let the completed leaf dry overnight or in a warm place for a few hours. A design can be partly formed, left to dry and worked on again by very quickly running it under the tap.

7 Creating tendrils

For the vine leaf design, tendrils are created with very thin lengths of natural round lace. Dampen the lace, wrap it tightly round a pencil, tape in place if necessary, and leave to dry. Add a small amount of PVA to the water used for damping to strengthen the lace. For extra strength, you can also paint a layer of PVA onto the back of the finished leaf when still damp.

8 Polishing

When the corsage is completely dry, it can be waxed and polished. Try not to lose any of the detail by rubbing too hard.

Two-tone Effect

Consider laminating two different colours of goatskin together with PVA glue (see page 18). When the leaf edges are curled and worked, flashes of the colour beneath will be subtly visible.

9 Finishing

Cut a small square of leather to hold the back pin in place. Pare the leather down to remove the bulk. Glue the pin in place with superglue, and place the covering leather between the bar and pin for extra security, sandwiching the tendrils in between, if using. You can attach two leaves together with a piece of twisted thonging lace, glued securely to the back.

Templates

Please note that the templates are reduced to either 25% or 50% of the original size and will need to be enlarged to reinstate the image at full size. Seam allowances are 1cm (⅜in) unless otherwise stated.

Plaited Cuff

(see page 24)

Enlarge by 400%

Butterfly Desk Set

(see page 28)

Enlarge by 400%

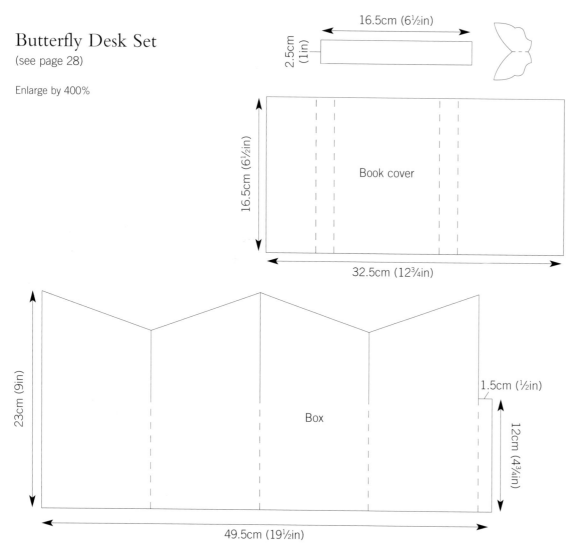

Coin Concertina

(see page 32)

Enlarge by 400%

Origami Box

(see page 36)

Enlarge by 400%

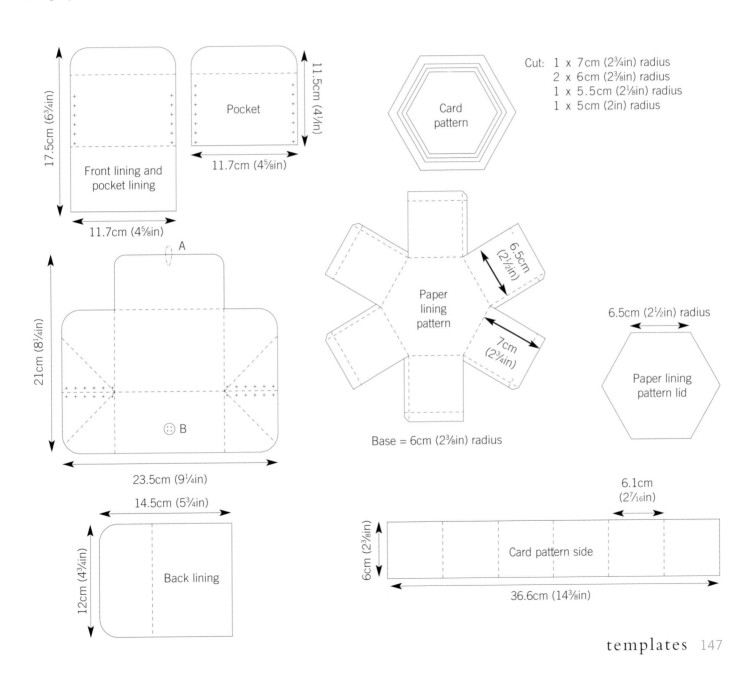

Coin Concertina

17.5cm (6¾in)

Pocket

11.5cm (4½in)

Front lining and pocket lining

11.7cm (4⅝in)

11.7cm (4⅝in)

A

21cm (8¼in)

B

23.5cm (9¼in)

14.5cm (5¾in)

12cm (4¾in)

Back lining

Origami Box

Card pattern

Cut: 1 x 7cm (2¾in) radius
2 x 6cm (2⅜in) radius
1 x 5.5cm (2⅛in) radius
1 x 5cm (2in) radius

6.5cm (2½in)

Paper lining pattern

7cm (2¾in)

Base = 6cm (2⅜in) radius

6.5cm (2½in) radius

Paper lining pattern lid

6.1cm (2⁷⁄₁₆in)

6cm (2⅜in)

Card pattern side

36.6cm (14⅜in)

Stripy Purse

(see page 50)

Enlarge by 400%

1.5cm (½in)

2.5cm (1in)

11cm (4¼in)

22cm (8½in)

18.5cm (7¼in)

Sandal Style (see page 54) and Moroccan Slippers (see page 110)

Enlarge by 400%

Size 6

Strap tucks under

Strap tucks under

A

B

A

B

Metallic lining to here

Upper and lining to here

Front strap x 1

Cut second ankle strap 45cm (17¾in) long

18cm (7in)

3cm (1¼in)

1cm (⅜in)

Pretty in Pink

(see page 58)

Enlarge by 800%

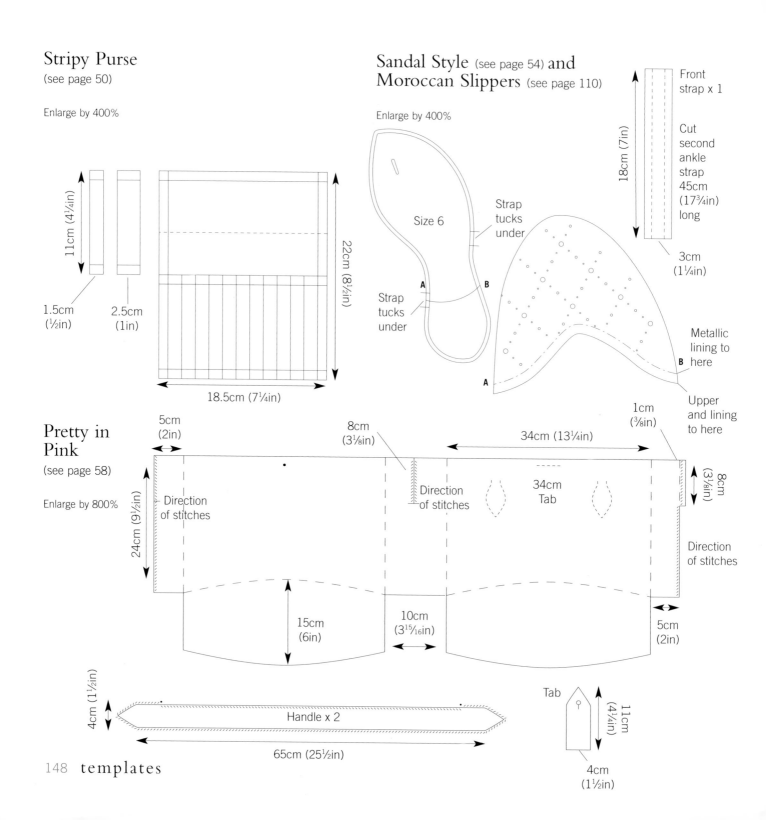

5cm (2in)

8cm (3⅛in)

34cm (13¼in)

Direction of stitches

Direction of stitches

34cm Tab

8cm (3⅛in)

Direction of stitches

24cm (9½in)

15cm (6in)

10cm (3¹⁵⁄₁₆in)

5cm (2in)

4cm (1½in)

Handle x 2

65cm (25½in)

Tab

11cm (4¼in)

4cm (1½in)

Disco Diva

(see page 66)

Enlarge by 400%

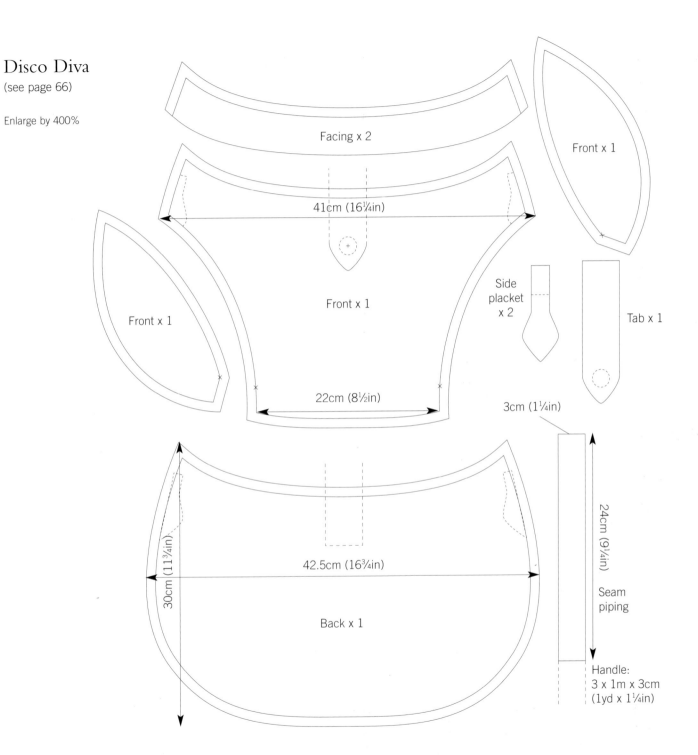

Facing x 2

41cm (16¼in)

Front x 1

Front x 1

Front x 1

22cm (8½in)

Side placket x 2

Tab x 1

3cm (1¼in)

30cm (11¾in)

42.5cm (16¾in)

Back x 1

24cm (9¼in)

Seam piping

Handle: 3 x 1m x 3cm (1yd x 1¼in)

Patent Belt (see page 78)

Belt length = 80 x 9cm (32 x 3½in)

Enlarge by 400%

A = 5 x 2cm
(2 x ¾in)

A x 1

B = 18 x 2.5cm (7 x 1in)

B x 1

C = 12 x 1.5cm
(4¾ x ½in)

C x 2

D = 8 x 3cm
(3⅛ x 1¼in)

D x 2

E = 12 x 3cm
(4¾ x 1¼in)

E x 1

F = 8 x 1.5cm
(3⅛ x ½in)

F x 2

G x 1

G = 31 x 3cm (12¼ x 1¼in)

H x 1

H = 22 x 3cm (8½ x 1¼in)

This diagram illustrates where to attach the metal fastenings to the various tabs in order to construct the belt.

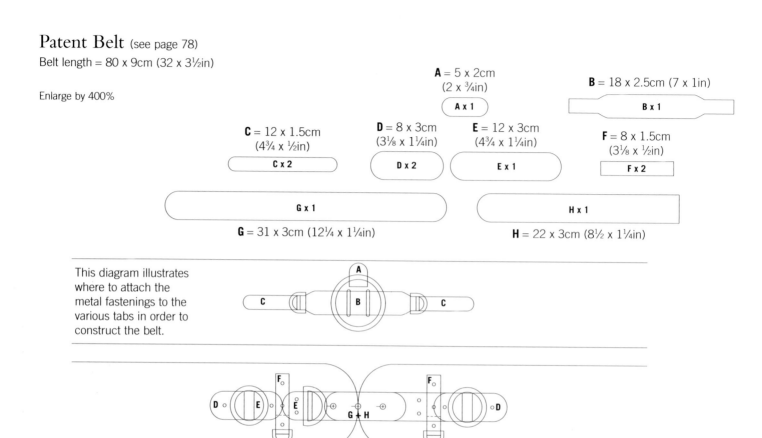

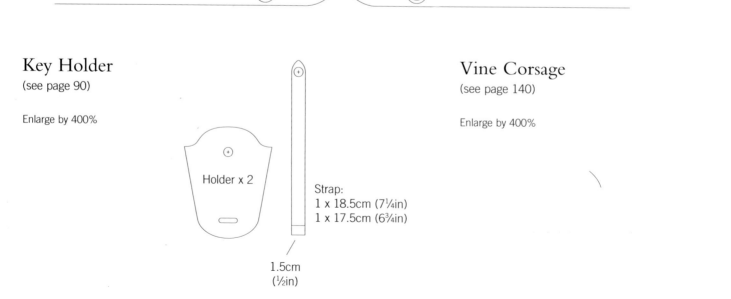

Key Holder

(see page 90)

Enlarge by 400%

Holder x 2

Strap:
1 x 18.5cm (7¼in)
1 x 17.5cm (6¾in)

1.5cm
(½in)

Vine Corsage

(see page 140)

Enlarge by 400%

Classic Duffel

(see page 82)

Enlarge by 400%

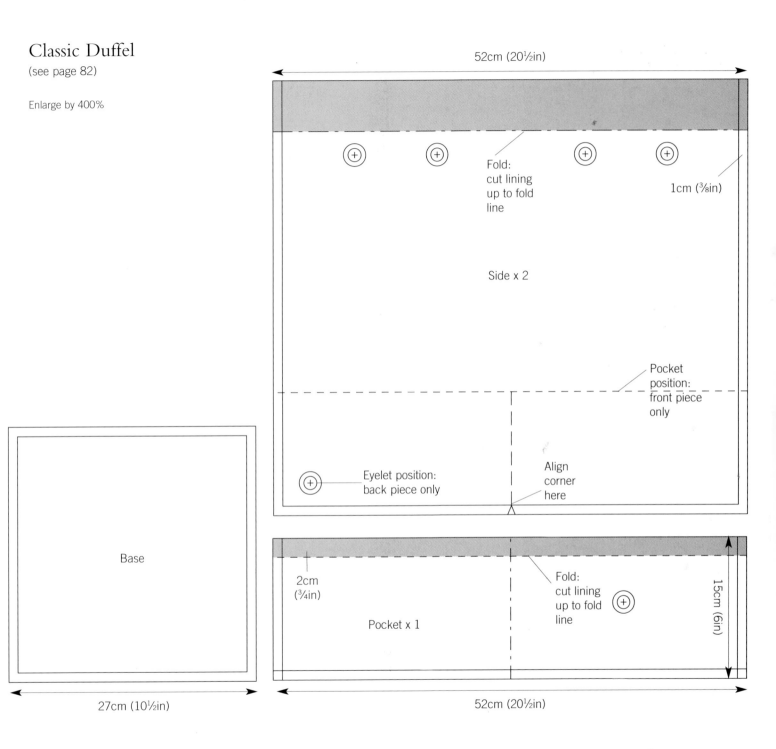

52cm (20½in)

Fold:
cut lining
up to fold
line

1cm (⅜in)

Side x 2

Pocket
position:
front piece
only

Eyelet position:
back piece only

Align
corner
here

Base

27cm (10½in)

2cm
(¾in)

Pocket x 1

Fold:
cut lining
up to fold
line

15cm (6in)

52cm (20½in)

Make-up Bag

(see page 86)

Enlarge by 400%

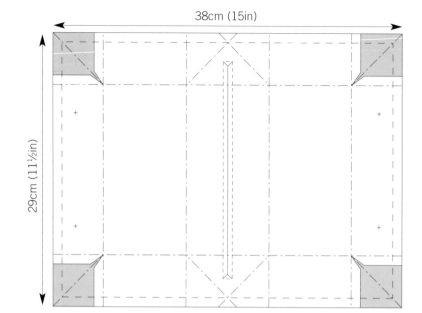

38cm (15in)

29cm (11½in)

Deco Bag

(see page 134)

Enlarge by 400%

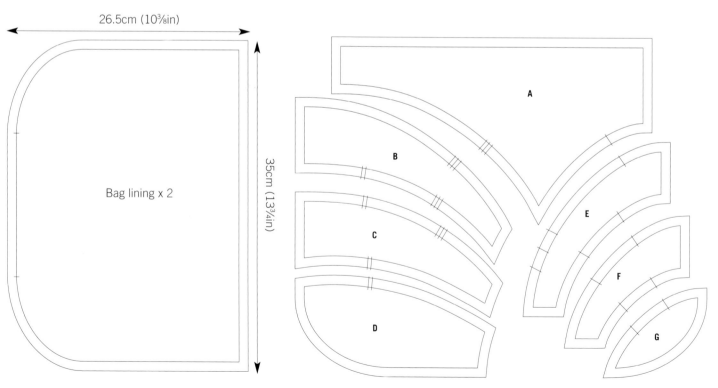

26.5cm (10⅜in)

35cm (13¾in)

Bag lining x 2

A

B

C

D

E

F

G

Record Bag

(see page 116)

Enlarge by 800%

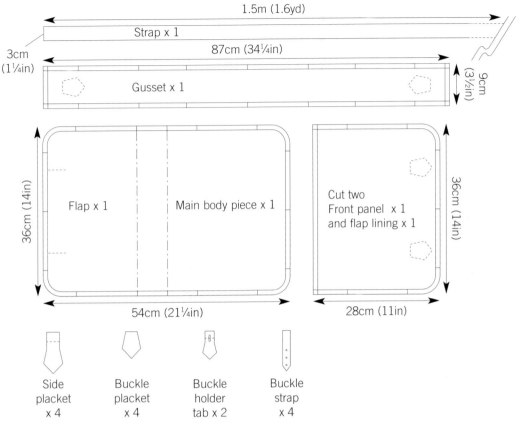

Strap x 1

1.5m (1.6yd)

3cm (1¼in)

87cm (34¼in)

9cm (3½in)

Gusset x 1

36cm (14in)

Flap x 1

Main body piece x 1

Cut two
Front panel x 1
and flap lining x 1

36cm (14in)

54cm (21¼in)

28cm (11in)

Side
placket
x 4

Buckle
placket
x 4

Buckle
holder
tab x 2

Buckle
strap
x 4

Braided Case

(see page 128)

Enlarge by 400%

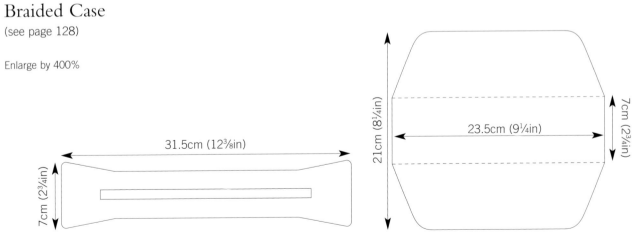

31.5cm (12⅜in)

7cm (2¾in)

21cm (8¼in)

23.5cm (9¼in)

7cm (2¾in)

Glossary

Bone: The action of using a bone folder to smooth and flatten leather, or the tool itself.

Burnishing: Polishing leather by rubbing with a cotton cloth, ideally undyed calico, or smooth piece of wood to create a shiny surface (vegetable-tanned leathers only).

Carving: Sometimes used alongside stamping, describes the action of cutting a pattern into the skin.

Chrome-tanned: Leather preserved using chrome salts, usually water-resistant fashion and lighter weight skins.

Clam: A saddler's clamp for holding work to be stitched by hand.

Crease (channelling, gouging, grooving): The action of cutting a channel or shallow groove into leather.

Cuir bouilli: An ancient method of moulding leather, implying the use of heat.

Embossing: An allover pattern created by use of a large metal plate, applied like stamping.

Flesh side: The underside of the leather.

Grain: The prominent texture of the surface of some leathers, especially goat. Full grain means a skin where the surface texture has not been altered in any way.

Grain side: The surface, or top side, of the leather.

Hide: A large full skin – usually cow.

Lacing fork: A pronged tool with straight teeth used to mark the holes for lacing or thonging.

Moulding: Forming wet vegetable-tanned leather into three-dimensional shapes, either by hand or by stretching over a former or mould.

Nappa: A full grain sheepskin.

Pare, paring (skive, skiving): Shaving the underside of leather to make it thinner (usually only along the edges).

Placket: I have called the piece of leather which supports a buckle or fastening a 'placket'. It may more properly be known as a billet or tab.

Pricking iron (stitching fork): A pronged tool with angled teeth used to mark the holes for hand stitching.

Punch: A metal tool used to make holes.

Russet: Vegetable-tanned hide with no dye or wax applied. The sheepskin version of this is known as 'basil'.

Shoulder: The top section of a hide.

Side: Half a large hide, usually cow or horse.

Skin: A small full skin, usually sheep, goat or calf.

Splitting, split: Splitting describes the action of shaving a whole skin or hide to remove a layer and make it thinner. A 'split' refers to a piece of leather produced from the underneath layer (without the top grain).

Stamping: Applying an impressed decoration to the surface of leather, by heat or pressure. Stamping in this book refers to the use of small metal stamps applied by hand or machine. This is also sometimes called 'tooling'.

Thonging (lacing): The use of flat or round strips of leather to decorate and join the edges of a leather item.

Vegetable-tanned: Leather preserved using vegetable matter such as bark, sumac and other tannin-rich plants.

Webbing: Woven fabric bands used for belts and handles.

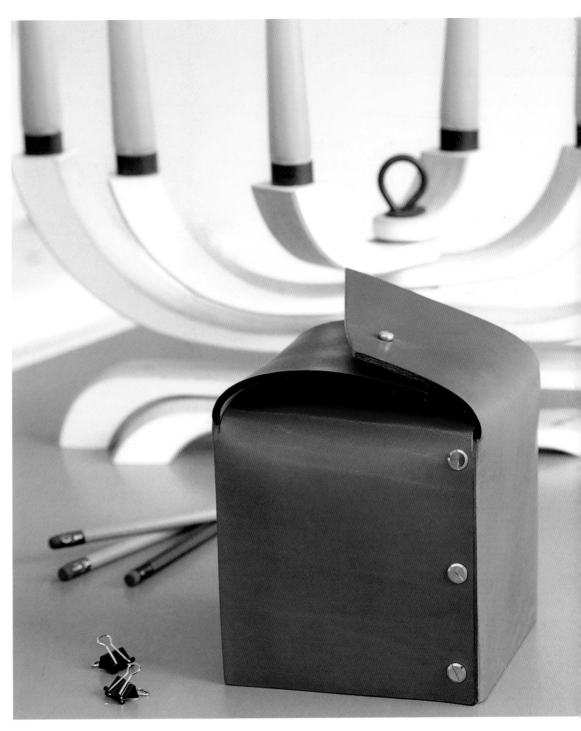

Resources

Courses/Further Study

Katherine Pogson is director of Designer Courses, where she teaches short courses in leather fashion accessories, glove-making and handbag design.

Designer Courses
www.designercourses.com
info@designercourses.com

Leather

Walter Reginald Group Ltd
Unit 6, 100 The Highway
London, E1W 2BX
Tel: 020 7481 2233
www.walterreginald.com
Very wide range of leathers in different weights and finishes.

GH Leathers Ltd
GH Leather
Units D and E
Bury Close
Higham Ferrers
Northants, NN10 8HQ
Tel: 01933 311116
www.leathermerchants.com
Specialize in lighter weight fashion leathers, suede and exotics.

Harmatan and Oakridge Leathers Ltd
Westfields Avenue
Higham Ferrers
Northamptonshire,
NN10 8AX
Tel: 01933 412151
www.harmatan.co.uk
Fine goatskin and calfskin bookbinding leathers.

Leather, tools and equipment

J Hewit & Sons Ltd
12 Nettlehill Road
Houstoun Industrial Estate
Livingston, EH54 5DL
Tel: 01506 444160
www.hewit.com
Bookbinding leathers, adhesives and equipment.

JT Batchelor Ltd
9–10 Culford Mews
Off Ball's Pond Road
London, N1 4DZ
Tel: 020 7254 2962
Good for tools, equipment, fittings and vegetable-tanned cowhides.

Tandy Leather Factory UK
Unit 2 Crofton Oak
North Portway Close
Round Spinney Industrial Estate
Northampton, NN3 8RD
Tel: 01604 647910
www.tandyleatherfactory.co.uk
Tools, equipment, fittings and some leather.

Metal fittings

Le Prevo
1 Charlotte Square
Newcastle upon Tyne
NE1 4XF
Tel: 0191 232 4179
www.leprevo.co.uk
Metal fittings, tools, equipment, dyes and finishes.

Bowstock Ltd
6 Mill Lane
North Tawton
Devon, EX20 2EE
Tel: 01562 746316
www.bowstock.co.uk
Metal fittings, tools, equipment, dyes and finishes.

S & K Leathergoods & Fittings Ltd
Unit GB
Leroy House
436 Essex Rd
London, N1 3QP
Tel: 020 7354 4435
www.skfittings.co.uk
Metal fittings.

Other supplies, tools and equipment

www.u-handbag.com
Very good selection of handles and frames, as well as linings, interfacings and patterns.

Kleins
5 Noel Street
London W1F 8GD
Tel: 020 7437 6162
www.kleins.co.uk
Bag and purse frames, haberdashery, buckles, clasps, trimmings.

MacCulloch and Wallis
25-26 Poland Street
London, W1F 8QN
Tel: 020 7629 0311
www.macculloch-wallis.co.uk
Fashion fabrics, haberdashery and sewing machines. Good for silks, linings, zips and trims.

William Gee
520–522 Kingsland Road
London, E8 4AR
Tel: 020 7254 2451
www.williamgee.co.uk

Wholesaler of fashion fabrics and trimmings – very good value.

Barnet Lawson
16–17 Little Portland Street
London, W1W 8NE
Tel: 020 7636 8591
www.bltrimmings.com
Haberdashery and trimmings.

Russell & Chapple
30-31 Store Street
London, WC1E 7QE
Tel: 020 7836 7521
www.russellandchapple.co.uk
E: info@randc.net
Canvas and other natural fabrics suitable for backing.

Shepherds Bookbinders Ltd
30 Gillingham Street
Victoria
London, SW1V 1HU
Tel: 020 7233 9999
www.bookbinding.co.uk
Japanese papers, bone folders and bookbinding equipment.

Alec Tiranti Ltd
27 Warren Street
London, W1T 5NB
Tel: 020 7380 0808
www.tiranti.co.uk
Mould making and sculpture materials supplies.

L Cornelissen & Son
105 Great Russell Street
London, WC1B 3RY
Tel: 020 7636 1045
www.cornelissen.com
Specialist supplier of art materials – brushes, paints, pigments.

USA

Tandy Leather Factory Inc.
1900 SE Loop 820
Fort Worth TX 76140
www.tandyleatherfactory.com
US Phone: 1-800-433-3201
International Phone:
1-817-496-4874
Canada Phone:
1-800-450-3062
UK Phone: 01604 647910
Leather, tools, equipment and finishes.

Dualoy
45 West 34th Street. Ste. 811
New York NY 10001
Tel: 212 736 3360
www.dualoy.com

Canada

Perfect Leather
555 King St W
Toronto, ON, M5V 1M1
Tel: 416-205-9775
Leather merchants.

Index

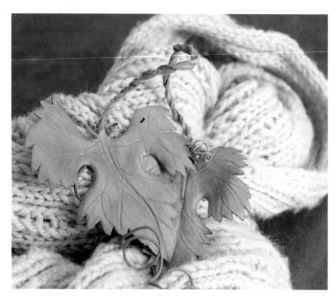

ACKNOWLEDGEMENTS

Warm thanks to Laydy for her enthusiastic, practical and creative support, and the loan of her beautiful fingers.

Thanks also to Patricia Hopewell for putting up with us so graciously when we hijacked her working environment.

Much love and gratitude to Paul for his nurturing and domestic talents, without which this book would have taken twice as long.

Lastly, I would like to thank Neil MacGregor and Valerie Michael for their warmth, generosity and inspiration when I first set out to explore the possibilities of leather design.

Photography by Holly Jolliffe. Illustrations by John Turner. Templates by Kang Chen.